CHOOSING PLAN A IN A PLAN B WORLD

Living Out the Lordship of Christ

JERRY WHITE

NAVPRESS

A MINISTRY OF THE NAVIGATORS

P.O. Box 6000, Colorado Springs, Colorado 80934

The Navigators is an international Christian organization.
Jesus Christ gave His followers the Great Commission to
go and make disciples (Matthew 28:19). The aim of The
Navigators is to help fulfill that commission by multiply-
ing laborers for Christ in every nation.

NavPress is the publishing ministry of The Navigators.
NavPress publications are tools to help Christians grow.
Although publications alone cannot make disciples or
change lives, they can help believers learn biblical discipleship, and apply what they learn to their lives and
ministries.

© 1986 by Jerry White
All rights reserved, including translation
Library of Congress Catalog Card Number: 86-63650
ISBN 08910-91416

Second printing, 1987

Printed in the United States of America

Contents

To
Lorne C. Sanny
in appreciation of his leadership
of The Navigators for thirty years,
his personal friendship to me,
and his lifelong example
of living and leading
under the lordship of Jesus Christ.

Author

Jerry White is General Director of The Navigators. He first came in contact with The Navigators as a student at the University of Washington. He maintained close contact throughout his military career, and helped begin Navigator ministries at the United States Air Force Academy in 1964 and at Purdue University in 1966. He was a regional director in the United States for 10 years.

Jerry's 13½ years of active service in the Air Force included duty as a mission controller at Cape Canaveral during the most active phase of the U.S. space flight program. He resigned from active duty in 1973.

He served as associate professor of astronautics at the United States Air Force Academy for six years, and co-authored a nationally recognized textbook on astrodynamics. He holds a bachelor's degree in electrical engineering from the University of Washington, a master's degree in astronautics from the Air Force Institute of Technology, and a doctorate in astronautics from Purdue University.

In addition to *Choosing Plan A in a Plan B World,* Jerry has also written *Honesty, Morality, and Conscience; Making the Grade: A Guide to Excellence in College; The Church and the Parachurch: An Uneasy Marriage;* and *The Power of Commitment.* He and his wife, Mary, are the authors of *Your Job: Survival or Satisfaction* and *Friends and Friendship.*

The White family lives in Colorado Springs, Colorado.

Preface

I write this preface in the midst of a trip to Nigeria and Kenya. As I interact with Christian men and women, African and expatriate, I am challenged by their commitment to the lordship of Christ. They sacrifice daily to reach people for Christ. Yet even they struggle with the common issues of lordship.

No one is immune from the temptation to live for self rather than for the Lord. Daily we face the competition between God's plan and the world's plan. So we must choose. In the vernacular, do we choose Plan A—God's plan—or that which is second best—Plan B?

I finish this book with an admixture of fear and excitement. I fear writing presumptuously, knowing I have such a great need for more submission in lordship. As I write, I find my personal spiritual poverty exposed, yet I am growing.

I am excited about the potential power of men and women who make Christ Lord of the many facets of their lives. They can turn their world upside-down. They possess the potential to infuse fresh life into an anemic Christian community caught up in activities, programs, and self-centeredness. Only churches dominated by people surrendered to the lordship of Christ will ever reach the lost of our communities. Our weakness paralyzes us and prevents us from experiencing the real power of the Christian life.

As I wrote *The Power of Commitment*, I realized that I only scratched the surface of the implications of the lordship of Jesus Christ. This present book grew from that realization.

This book does not contain a full theology of the lordship of Christ. Rather it is a focus on the practical issues of lordship in daily living, a challenge to choose Plan A. Much more could be said on each subject. My purpose is to stimulate your thinking, to cause you to search the Scriptures and examine your life more thoroughly.

Use this book devotionally and prayerfully. Read it slowly. Wrestle with the implications. Argue with the validity. And above all, apply it to your life.

The greatest blight on the Church today is Christians whose lives do not reflect the lordship of Christ. May this volume be used by God to help cure that malady.

Jerry White

JESUS
IS
LORD

THEREFORE ALSO GOD HIGHLY EXALTED HIM . . .
THAT AT THE NAME OF JESUS EVERY
KNEE SHOULD BOW, OF THOSE WHO ARE IN
HEAVEN, AND ON EARTH, AND UNDER THE
EARTH, AND THAT EVERY TONGUE SHOULD
CONFESS THAT JESUS CHRIST IS LORD.
Philippians 2:9-10

1
He Is Lord . . . Or Is He?

Picture the scene: a small group of Christians gather in a home, enjoying a great time of fellowship and Bible study. They join hands and sing:

> He is Lord, He is Lord.
> He is risen from the dead, and He is Lord.
> Every knee shall bow, every tongue confess
> That Jesus Christ is Lord.

They repeat the song. A few eyes close. Goose bumps rise. They *feel* worshipful and spiritual.

As they leave, nagging doubts cross their minds. Did they sing a lie? Does simply singing or saying "He is Lord" make it so? Certainly Jesus *is* Lord. God made Him such. Whether we believe it or respond to His lordship, the fact remains eternally true. In God's perfect time, all humankind will acknowledge it.

But how do we match what we say with what we do in life? Surely Christ's lordship is more than mere words.

We see the disparity between our words and the feelings deep in our hearts. As we go through the motions of outward spiritual life, we feel guilty knowing that Christ's lordship still remains unresolved in our hearts and lives. In the early years of our Christian growth we are sensitive to the difference, and we struggle to close the gap. Later we may become callous, telling ourselves we must just live with the disparity. We may become completely insensitive to Christ's lordship, or excuse our insensitivity by the thought that the closer we get to God, the more sin we will see in our lives. We go on saying the right things, unaware that Christ's lordship is not real to us at all.

Two words in Philippians 2:9-10 help us recover that sensitivity: they are *Lord* and *confess.*

The Scriptures use the title "Lord" repeatedly in referring to Jesus. The Greek word *kurios* means an owner who has control of all his possessions (as in Matthew 20:8, the owner of a vineyard). It also means "master," the one to whom service is due. It can mean emperor or king, or simply be a title of respect. In the New Testament, *kurios* or *Lord* is the Septuagint translation of the Old Testament word for Jehovah. In the epistles, the word becomes an exclusive title of God or of Jesus.

So Jesus is Owner, Master, and King. He reigns over all. The Scriptures distinguish Him from the many lords, kings, and masters of the earth. He is King of kings, and Lord of lords. Revelation 19:16 speaks of His coming reign: "And on His robe and on His thigh He has a name written, 'King of kings, and Lord of lords.'" He stands above all powers and potentates.

But is He Lord, Owner, and Master of our lives? This is where His lordship counts for us—in the private halls of our inner beings. It is there we "confess" Him as Lord.

Confessing Christ as Lord means much more than repeating a few words or singing spiritual-sounding phrases, even with feeling. It is more than admitting to a fact. It is to *admit* and *submit*. We admit that Christ is Lord and submit our lives to His lordship. The Bible uses the word *confess* in just that manner. Confession is intimately related to believing. The Apostle Paul declared:

> If you confess with your mouth Jesus as Lord, and believe in your heart that God raised Him from the dead, you shall be saved; for with the heart man believes, resulting in righteousness, and with the mouth he confesses, resulting in salvation. (Romans 10:9-10)

As in salvation, external words require internal belief. In confession of lordship, too, both are necessary. The word *confess* means, however, more than mental assent. "[Confess] implies a decision to pledge oneself in loyalty to Jesus Christ as Lord in response to the Holy Spirit."[1]

We *admit* (or confess) that Jesus Christ is the Messiah, that He died and rose from the dead, and that our only hope of salvation is in Him. In salvation we *submit* to Him as we surrender our lives. In lordship we *admit* that Jesus is Lord and Master and we *submit* to that lordship in our hearts and in our daily lives.

Only in the free societies of the world can we confess His lordship publicly with little or no consequence. In New Testament times, confessing Christ as Lord meant an irreversible change of public life. There were no cheap confessions, no ceremonial declarations of lordship.

So we confess:

> publicly before men—privately in our hearts,
> with our tongues—with our hearts,
> admitting facts of lordship—living actions of lordship,
> admitting His lordship—submitting to His lordship.

All the mental understanding in the world will never suffice for the true decision of lordship that will forever change the direction and focus of the "average" Christian. We wrestle with the concept. We struggle with its implications. We say the words and find our weakness in the daily battle to make it real. Even when, in tears, we submit in moments of consecration, we still need to grapple with specific issues of His lordship.

In the chapters that follow I attempt to help each of us in that pilgrimage to full submission to the lordship of Jesus Christ. As the Apostle Paul said:

> Brethren, I do not regard myself as having laid hold of it yet; but one thing I do: forgetting what lies behind and reaching forward to what lies ahead, *I press on toward the goal* for the prize of the upward call of God in Christ Jesus. (Philippians 3:13-14)

What greater goal than to live completely under Christ's loving lordship? In comparison, all other goals fade into insignificance. Discover the joy of knowing Him as Lord in the reality of life.

NOTE:
   1. *The New Testament Dictionary* (Grand Rapids: Eerdmans, 1962), page 247.

AND WHY DO YOU CALL ME "LORD, LORD,"
AND DO NOT DO WHAT I SAY?
Luke 6:46

2
Obedience:
The Proof of Lordship

A frantic pounding on our door interrupted the serenity of our first day on Maui, Hawaii. "You've got to evacuate!" the manager shouted. "A *tsunami* is coming in one hour!"

I thought he was joking. I didn't even know what a *tsunami* was. I soon learned that it's a tidal wave.

An earthquake of 7.7 magnitude had shaken the Aleutian Islands off Alaska, and its shock began a tidal wave that was rushing toward Hawaii, scheduled to arrive at 5:06 p.m. In the late 1800s a 100-foot tidal wave struck with tragic destruction. In 1957 a 40-foot wave rushed onto Kauai.

Bitter experience taught the Islanders to treat such warnings with great respect. But what about us tourists? I didn't see how it could occur. The ocean appeared to be so calm. Yet I realized it could happen.

So we grabbed a few items—a jacket, water, a Bible, another book, *and* my peanut M & M's! We drove to high ground, and there we sat with dozens of other people for several hours, glued to the radio. After five or six initial waves only a few feet high came in fifteen-minute intervals, the danger passed and an "all clear" was given by the emergency broadcast system. The *tsunami* had bypassed the Islands.

During the emergency experts rushed to the control point of information in Diamond Head crater. Observations were made. Experience was drawn upon. Interview after interview revealed one startling fact: no one really knew what would happen. All predictions were educated guesses.

Maybe I should have ignored the warnings and stayed on the beach, I thought. But I know that failure to obey could have resulted in great calamity. I have tried to analyze why I even considered not obeying the command to evacuate. Upon reflection, the reasons mirror my reluctance to obey God.

I react against *anyone* telling me what to do. Something within me rebels at any invasion of my will that requires me to obey. I want to decide. I want to volunteer. I want the option. Even when God speaks, my first response is to refuse. It must be the impulse of our first father, Adam, when confronted by God's command, "but from the tree of the knowledge of good and evil you shall not eat" (Genesis 2:17). Children exhibit the tendency to do the exact opposite of what they are told to do. Mother says, "Bobby, don't touch that stove. It will burn you." So what does Bobby do? He touches the stove and learns a painful lesson. So often this is our response to God's commands.

A second response is, *I want to argue the merits of obedience.* Are you sure the *tsunami* warning is accurate? How do you know? Can't we just stay here a little longer until we know for sure? I challenge the accuracy and wisdom of the command. I want all the facts, and then *I will make my decision.* Far be it from me to take someone else's word! I want you to prove it. Show me!

Such arrogance is an affront to the lordship of Christ. In love He speaks to me through His Word, warning me of so many things. Yet I argue, examine, and negotiate. I question His authority and wisdom. I treat Christ as an adversary rather than a friend, even though He said, "You are My friends, if you do what I command you" (John 15:14). He always commands with my best interests at heart.

A third response: *I must understand why before I obey.* Would you explain how a tidal wave can be set off by an Alaskan earthquake? What are the physics of the wave? Why is the greatest danger in the third or fourth wave? I hurled all of these questions at the manager while others were yet to be warned. How foolish!

In a similar way I question many of Christ's commands. I don't see a clear reason for the command, so I want to delay obedience until I understand. But God does not always offer explanations for every command. He asks us to simply trust that He knows what is best for us. Then as we obey, we see His wisdom.

Christians may ask, "How could premarital sex hurt anyone, if love is there?" God commands us to abstain until marriage. Only later, often too late, does one see fully the wisdom and consequences of obedience. God does not explain the "why" but simply offers His holiness as the reason. And so it is in many areas of life: we obey now and understand later. I do not advocate blind, unthinking obedience to man's fallible codes of conduct, but loving, responsive obedience to the Lord Jesus in clear issues of His Word. They are few, but clear.

A final response: *I am not sure the results of obedience will really be to my benefit.* What if someone burglarizes the condo while I am running to high ground? What if I lose my books—and my little portable computer? There are no answers, or guarantees, to all of these "what ifs." I obey to save my life. I can never know the outcome for sure until I obey. In obedience I place myself completely in God's hands.

God does not bribe us into obedience. Yes, blessing is promised to the obedient. But what kind of blessing? For many Christians in centuries past obedience led to persecution and death. Peter and the other apostles affirmed the obvious, but difficult principle: "We must obey God rather than men" (Acts 5:29). They put their lives into God's hands. The lordship of Christ became reality as they obeyed.

The ultimate evidence of the lordship of Christ lies in obedience, both of action and heart. There can be no true lordship without obedience. From the beginning of time obedience has been God's touchstone of love.

"Now if you obey me fully . . ." (Exodus 19:5, NIV).
"Obey Him with all your heart and soul" (Deuteronomy 30:2).
"If anyone loves Me, he will keep My word" (John 14:23).
In passage after passage God emphasizes obedience—
not for solutions, but for fellowship,
not for earning grace, but for exercising lordship.

To acknowledge Christ as Lord means to obey Him implicitly as Lord. But why? Why should we obey at all? To make life easier for us? Out of fear? No. Obey in response to the love of Christ in His consummate sacrifice on the cross. Isaac Watts' familiar words express it best.

> Alas! and did my Savior bleed
>   And did my sovereign die?
> Would He devote that sacred Head
>   For sinners such as I?

Was it for sins that I have done
He suffered on the tree?
Amazing pity! grace unknown!
And love beyond degree!

But drops of grief can ne'er repay
The debt of love I owe:
Here, Lord, I give my self away—
'Tis all that I can do.
                                —Isaac Watts

Should we do less than fully submit ourselves to Christ's loving lordship? Should we do less than obey?

3
The Cost of Lordship

"Send in for your free sample."

"No money down. No payments for two years."

"Don't buy anything. Just register to win a free vacation in Hawaii."

"Two nights free in beautiful mountain resort. Call this number to reserve your time."

Human motives always respond to getting something free. But we all know that those wonderful offers always have a catch—a hidden angle. Someone wants to sell something. There is always a cost. And that which is worthwhile usually costs more. Nothing is free. Someone always pays.

Salvation is free to us only because Jesus Christ paid the price of our redemption from sin. We receive grace, freely given, totally undeserved. It is truly a gift with no strings attached.

But what about lordship? Does commitment to the lordship of Christ involve a cost? Yes, it does.

Thinking persons may say that they have been deceived—free salvation, but costly lordship. God offers salvation by grace with no hidden price. Then suddenly the concept of lordship, commitment, and sacrifice surface to confront the new believer. Isn't this a contradiction—free, but costly? Is it just like the tricks of modern marketing, something free up front, with great cost later?

We receive salvation and live a victorious Christian life completely by grace. We earn neither. God Himself is the source of both.

Our problem lies with the term "cost." Our experience in commerce gives the word "cost" a totally negative connotation. We may respond by thinking that "it costs too much and is not worth it." We picture the reluctant payment for goods or services.

First, when we use the term here, "cost" does not mean money. Instead, we mean making choices in the conduct of our lives. These choices usually involve some type of exchange, such as time or activities.

Perhaps something similar happened in your courtship. Night after night, day after day for weeks on end you spent your spare time with your loved one—at great cost. Hobbies languished. Exercise programs floundered. Other friendships were put on hold. Jobs suffered. Yet your great desire to be together made the sacrifices of no consequence. To say it involved "cost" would be ridiculous. You *wanted* the relationship more than anything else. Yet an outside observer might note the great cost you paid in that courtship.

If you are married and have children, you have another beautiful picture. Children are expensive in terms of money, energy, and time. Before you had a child, you may have known some of the cost. Yet you would never trade one of those blessed children for all the money and time you would have saved.

So it is with the cost of lordship. We make choices that result in a relationship with Christ, which is beyond value. What appears to be a sacrifice to others we hardly notice.

So why all this talk about "costly lordship"? It is because we always seem to weigh the impact of decision and choices *before* we make them. They look like sacrifice. They seem hard. They call for surrender and submission to Christ. We are deceived into thinking that we will suffer loss and feel the pain of giving something up, although the opposite is the case. To keep the habit, the passions, the self-serving activity would actually lead to great pain and spiritual harm.

Jim Elliot once said, "He is no fool who gives what he cannot keep to gain what he cannot lose." Obedience and lordship are never painful after we choose them. The pain is only during the time of decision.

Luke 14:28-30 describes the costly process of discipleship:

> For which one of you, when he wants to build a tower, does not first sit down and calculate the cost, to see if he has enough to complete it? Otherwise, when he has laid a foundation, and is not able to finish, all who observe it begin to ridicule him, saying, "This man began to build and was not able to finish."

Jesus teaches that there can be no halfway or halfhearted choices. He challenges mindless decisions. Think, He says. Count the cost. Understand the implications.

Jesus challenges incomplete lordship. Christians who talk lordship but don't follow through become a laughingstock of the nonChristian community. Jesus wants clear, intelligent, permanent choices.

So what does this mean practically? The cost varies for

each person. For one, it costs possessions. For another, money. For another, time, or reputation, or position, or recreation. There is no list of "lordship commodities." To give up smoking tobacco is no lordship decision at all for me, because I don't smoke. Yet for one who is addicted and is convicted to stop, it is a big issue. One person may need to reduce drastically the amount of time spent watching television. But others, who watch very little, find that no cost. Lordship decisions are not always a response to sin. They can involve the most innocent of activities, such as hobbies or recreation.

 So what are some of the costs that will confront us as we struggle with decisions of lordship?

First we must deal with issues of *sin*. Even though many lordship choices are not issues of sin, the first line of decisions must deal with those that are sin. But is this a cost? Only in the mind. A carnal Christian's mind *pictures* that giving up sin will somehow be a loss to his happiness. This is Satan's deception. The reality is that sin eats like a festering sore and constantly works at destroying spiritual vitality. Sin never gives happiness. So abandoning the sin under the lordship of Christ is no cost; it is a great relief. Yet these lordship choices must be made. And for some, the choice will be difficult, because the bond to the sin is so strong.

A second set of issues has to do with *possessions*. Jesus said, "So therefore, no one of you can be My disciple who does not give up all his own possessions" (Luke 14:33). Possessions can stand between us and the effective lordship of Christ in our lives. There are three issues—having possessions, grasping possessions, and lusting for possessions. Although this issue is addressed in another chapter, we need to focus on it briefly here.

We can be preoccupied by possessions even when we do not have them. We can lust—deeply long for—possessions and thus not be surrendered to Christ's lordship. We can grasp the possessions we have and selfishly cling to them so that they begin to control our lives, subverting the lordship of Christ. In other circumstances we neither grasp nor lust for possessions, but we simply own them. In most cases, that poses no problem. However, in some circumstances our possessions—their kind, their beauty, the amount—may offend the people around us, whom we wish to reach for Christ. One act of lordship may be to give up these possessions, even when our heart toward them is right. The sense of Luke 14:33 is that we are to "give up our right to" our possessions.

A significant lordship choice concerns the use of our *time*. Whatever we do costs time. We use time to serve either ourselves or others. As we grow in Christ, we are faced with choices. Will we choose to sacrifice to spend time on those things that God wants rather than on our own pursuits? It will involve a cost, because we exchange one use of time for another. We may need to work fewer hours, spend less time in leisure, and spend more time in Bible study, or spend some time with nonChristians.

There are many other areas of perceived cost—hobbies, recreation, promotions, geographical location, profession. They all must come under the lordship of Christ. Our willingness to incur the cost, with joy, will result in God's ultimate blessing upon us.

Lest we settle too easily on the concept that all cost of lordship is perceived rather than real, we need to consider the possibility of actual persecution for our faith. In many parts of the world the results of lordship decisions may be imprisonment, loss of jobs, financial loss, family separations, and difficult circumstances. History reveals that discipleship and lordship have often been very costly in real terms. But those under persecution testify that they would make no other choice. The rewards of following our Lord far outweigh the cost.

Whether the cost of lordship is perceived or real, it is still a cost. And we must choose, regardless of the cost. No cost is too great to reap the rewards of living under the lordship of Jesus Christ.

THE SON OF MAN IS LORD EVEN OF THE SABBATH.
Mark 2:28

4
Legalism:
The Enemy of Lordship

Do you remember laughing over those outrageous laws still on the books in some cities? Like, it's illegal to walk a pig across the street on Saturdays in Podunksville! We laugh and wonder how anyone could seriously make such ridiculous laws. Then we look back on some Christian "laws" of the past century—and laugh a little less loudly, but still wonder how anyone could seriously have proposed them: no mixed bathing, no shopping on Sunday, no jewelry or makeup for women, no shaving for married men. The Christian who ridiculed these customs experienced considerable pressure to conform or was excluded from close spiritual fellowship.

Jesus regularly encountered—and withstood—similar issues. Among the Jews keeping the Sabbath was a major issue. It governed their lives almost as rigidly as Monday Night Football in the U.S. governs the lives of some people. The keeping of the Sabbath was the ultimate mark of a faithful Jew. From sundown Friday to sundown Saturday faithful Jews celebrated the sacred Sabbath. Rituals of family worship and the prohibition against any work controlled the day. Even when the Jews were captives in a foreign land, observing the Sabbath gave them a sense of identity and dignity as a people.

Jesus showed that God's intention for the Sabbath had been obscured by legalistic rules. Three gospels (Matthew 12:1-8, Mark 2:23-28, Luke 6:1-5) record the incident of the grainfields. The disciples were hungry, so as they walked through the field, they stripped grain off the standing stems and ate it. The Pharisees were there to confront them. Jesus directly answered these "enforcers," using King David as an example. Hungry and weary from battle, David entered the House of God and ate the consecrated bread.

Jesus stated both a principle of the Sabbath and of any legalistic rule: "The Sabbath was made for man, and not man for the Sabbath. Consequently, the Son of Man is Lord even of the Sabbath" (Mark 2:27-28).

Later the Pharisees tested Jesus by seeing whether He would heal a man with a withered hand on the Sabbath. Jesus did heal him, challenging them, "Is it lawful on the Sabbath to do good or to do harm, to save a life or to kill?" (Mark 3:4). Jesus tried to break through their tradition to the heart of what God intended.

Through the centuries people have built up traditions, rules, and laws to govern the activities of Christians. Human beings gravitate to rules so they do not have to think for themselves. We at once both resist and value the rules. We resist rules because we tend to rebel against any restraint; we value rules because they provide boundaries for conduct—

whether or not we intend to observe them.

Living under grace is almost too great a freedom. Thus churches and other Christian groups set up various rule systems for Christian conduct. We may laugh at the puritanical practices of the past, but we also need to examine the rules we impose today, which may be laughed at by the next generation.

At this point it would be easy to embark on a "hit list" of rules and traditions that need to be destroyed, but that would be fruitless. It would make some of you angry—both at what was on the list and what was not. We all have our favorite excesses and our favorite touchstones of external fidelity to Christian living.

The issue is deeper, much deeper, than specific rules. The real issue is *legalism*. Legalism systematically attacks and destroys the purity of the gospel. It substitutes rules for faith, traditions for spiritual thinking, boundaries for freedom, and law for grace.

Legalism often grows out of well-intentioned guidelines for living. A few godly people pray and seek God's will as to how they should live. They set certain patterns for themselves. Were it to end there, all would be well, but it doesn't. Usually they then impose those same guidelines on others, depriving them of the invaluable experience of seeking God for guidance in their own conduct.

Unfortunately, many of these legalistic rules have no clear biblical basis. Instead, they are secondary or derivative extensions of biblical principles—usually from passages on the care of the body, the weaker brother, or association with the world. They often become hopelessly confused with commonly held traditions of a specific culture.

Legalism obscures and confuses grace in the mind of the unbeliever causing him to live by law or fear, though saved by grace. He sees the rules and concludes that keeping them makes one a Christian. The unbeliever then either rejects the rules and turns away, or accepts them, becoming duped into believing that he is now saved.

Look around you at churches where the rites of membership blind people to the truth of grace. Think about the rituals of many cults. They all began with small excursions from the truth that seemed so harmless at the outset. Then they grew into rules and rites of fellowship.

Paul saw this so clearly in the Galatian church: "I am amazed that you are so quickly deserting Him who called you by the grace of Christ, for a different gospel" (Galatians 1:6). A different gospel? Was it not just a little dispute over circumcision and association with Gentiles? Didn't Paul overstate the case? No, he saw clearly that *anything* added to the gospel creates a different gospel.

Surely a believer could choose to be circumcised. It would do no harm. But soon his son or neighbor might be circumcised, thinking it was the ritual initiation into salvation. "Do not be subject again to a yoke of slavery" (Galatians 5:1), Paul declared, recognizing that the law enslaves. Only grace frees.

I can preach and teach on grace, but I am still a legalist at heart. My early Christian training stamped certain marks on my conscience that keep influencing me. Mary and I were married on Saturday night. But where was I Sunday morning? In church. Was that spiritual? No, it was probably stupid. I felt *constrained* (that's a good word for legalistic action) to go. I actually thought—though I never verbalized this— that God would be more pleased with me if I were in church. No exceptions.

One year later we were traveling in 100-degree heat in northern Texas, and Mary was six months pregnant. It was our anniversary. Where did we go that night? To church, of course—in a strange town, in misery. I was constrained! I was legalistic. It took some time for me to realize this and then to begin a process of change. Yet that change was necessary for me to grow in a deeper understanding of grace.

Every time I interact with my four children on issues of conduct I am torn between setting rules I think are right for their good and the danger of legalism. I remember many discussions on conduct for which I had *no* significant foundation. I meant well. I still do. And some restrictions are still in place. Yet I squirm as I write this for I see some of my own inconsistencies—and especially my history. I am still learning.

Jesus is Lord of the Sabbath and of all those rules that we allow to be placed upon us. When we live under His lordship, we freely choose to do or not do many things. We avoid sin and worldliness. We long for holiness. We want to be truly like Him. But we cannot force *someone else* to conform to our leading from Christ.

To leave the discussion here could create considerable confusion. Remember, the topic is legalism—any action, activity, or rule that I perceive will earn grace with God. But rules or rituals can never do that.

Are there rules that a group may accept as guidelines for conduct? Yes, but very carefully, rarely making them a test for fellowship. We do want to influence people to holy living, but not mandate the externals. We want to grow from internal conviction, not external rules.

When Christ is truly Lord of my life, I see others not according to their observance of rules, but by their spiritual hunger and growth. When there are actions or issues they should abandon, let it be like the shedding of a butterfly's cocoon—the natural outcome of growth.

AND I HAVE SEEN, AND HAVE BORNE WITNESS
THAT THIS IS THE SON OF GOD.
John 1:34

5
Firsthand Reality

"I won't believe it until I see it!" How many times have you heard that? How many times have I said it? Some things are too unbelievable for a secondhand report: marriage, a new baby, the first airplane flight, the first man on the moon.

I remember the early days of America's space program. As a young mission controller at Cape Canaveral, I daily watched rockets thunder off the launch pad and then gather speed to hurl objects into space. Yet when President Kennedy announced that we would place a man on the moon by the end of the 1960s, I thought, "I'll believe it when I see it!" It seemed an impossible task. But it happened, and we saw it on TV. My doubts were shattered by reality.

John the Baptist must have felt that way. He knew his

orders. He preached repentance. He knew he was paving the way for the Messiah. Each night he must have wondered, "When will He come? How will I know Him? What will He do?" Then one day the Messiah came, and at first John did not recognize Him. God had to tell him, "He upon whom you see the Spirit descending and remaining upon Him, this is the one who baptizes in the Holy Spirit" (John 1:33). John saw just that. "I have seen, and have borne witness that this is the Son of God" (John 1:34).

How could John describe the feelings he experienced or the reality of *knowing* that Jesus was the Messiah? Even the disciples would not fully realize that until much later. John the Baptist was the first to express the lordship of Christ: "He must increase, but I must decrease" (John 3:30).

One Christian cannot fully explain a lordship experience to another. There is no vicarious lordship, no secondhand living. It is something you must experience for yourself. It is a reality known only to those who place themselves under Christ's lordship.

This acceptance of lordship is not a second salvation, nor a second blessing. It is a serious life decision in which you yield lordship of your life to Christ. For some, this decision for lordship is made at the time of their salvation. Others, for a variety of reasons, never consciously make such a surrender. They are certain of salvation, yet Christ's lordship is not yet a reality for them. They live with their feet in both worlds—the world of flesh and the world of the Spirit.

Jesus' lordship is synonymous with the Holy Spirit's control of your life. His lordship extends to every action, thought, and motive. It opposes the carnal Christian life.

The majority of the epistles are written to Christians struggling with the lordship of Christ. No Christian denies the idea that Jesus *is* Lord, yet his life often denies the reality. We *admit* that Jesus is Lord, but we do not *submit*. It is this final step that breaks through the hard shell of our lives. We submit and openly acknowledge His lordship, privately *and* publicly.

In other cultures and earlier centuries, baptism expressed that profession of lordship. Today baptism is often reduced to an act without commitment, unrelated to lordship. Baptism is meant to be an identification with Christ, but we have often made it an identification with a human organization. There is more to baptism than lordship, but without lordship the meaning of baptism is greatly cheapened.

Believing in Christ's lordship is not enough. You need to experience it. Why not surrender your life now to the lordship of Christ? Do it by saying simply, "Lord, I know You are Lord of all. I admit that. Now I submit to Your lordship in every area of my life. I give You control from this time onward."

Take the first opportunity to share your commitment publicly—in church, in a small group, with a friend.

Enjoy incredible freedom and peace as Christ's lordship daily conforms your life to His image.

Welcome to the camp of the committed.

HE REBUKED THE WIND AND SAID TO THE SEA, "HUSH, BE STILL."
AND THE WIND DIED DOWN AND IT BECAME PERFECTLY CALM. AND
HE SAID TO THEM, "WHY ARE YOU SO TIMID? HOW IS IT THAT
YOU HAVE NO FAITH?" AND THEY BECAME VERY MUCH AFRAID AND
SAID TO ONE ANOTHER, "WHO THEN IS THIS, THAT EVEN THE WIND
AND THE SEA OBEY HIM?"
Mark 4:39-41

6
Nature:
Lordship Over His Creation

Early one morning in 1970, while I was staying in a friend's house in the Los Angeles area, he rushed into my bedroom and shook me awake. Though groggy, I realized the entire room—the entire house—was shaking. We ran out into the courtyard and stood away from the building, feeling the sickening tremble of the earth beneath us. An earthquake had disturbed the tranquility of that early morning.

We have come to accept "natural" disasters or occurrences as part of the mystery of the earth. But it is not nature that is powerful; it is God. The psalmist said it well: "Let the glory of the Lord endure forever; let the Lord be glad in His works; He looks at the earth, and it trembles; He touches the mountains, and they smoke" (Psalm 104:31-32).

God's actions cannot be predicted. As His creation, the earth still holds mysteries that have controlled the physical destiny of humankind for ages. Floods, hurricanes, tidal waves, volcanoes, blizzards, drought, and extreme cold or heat literally control our future. God is Master of it all. He speaks, and the earth moves. No one can predict the smallest, or largest, of its motions. Satellites and computers can only guess what will happen next. Our technical knowledge seems puny in comparison to the unpredictability of the earth's most natural actions.

Yet we fight the authority and lordship of God the Father and His Son, Jesus Christ. We try to find answers that lie only in God. We put our trust in science and technology, even when they can't foresee the simplest of the earth's capricious actions.

Centuries and generations have passed. Civilizations have been destroyed by one geological or meteorological occurrence after another. Yet man thinks he is supreme. How arrogant! How foolish! If only we could realize that God is the sovereign initiator in all creation, even of life itself. God passed this power to His Son, Jesus Christ.

> In the past God spoke to our forefathers through the prophets at many times and in various ways, but in these last days he has spoken to us by his Son, whom he appointed heir of all things, and through whom he made the universe. The Son . . . sustaining all things by his powerful word. (Hebrews 1:1-3, NIV)

Jesus Christ is the Lord of creation, the Lord of the earth. All things are under His hand. This does not mean that we should live in ignorance or foolish superstition. We can always be challenged by the unknowns of creation. We can study the creation and deeply appreciate the genius of God.

The lordship of Christ extends to every natural event. He is not ignorant of each quaking of the crust of the earth, each storm, and each molten stirring beneath the earth. Yet He has compassion and concern for each one caught in the conflagration of those natural events. Through such events He speaks to get our attention in a way that no other event can. He speaks out in the midst of human disaster to break through the hardened heart to show His love. Loss of life may occur, but what is of paramount importance is the possible loss of eternal life. The Lord Christ takes every means at His disposal to communicate that *He is Lord*—to cause us to acknowledge Him before it is too late.

His rule as Lord extends from east to west, from north to south, to the highest heights and deepest depths of the earth. Our confidence rests in His lordship over all natural events.

LORD
OF MY
EMOTIONS

AS SORROWFUL YET ALWAYS REJOICING.
2 Corinthians 6:10

FOR EVEN WHEN WE CAME INTO MACEDONIA
OUR FLESH HAD NO REST, BUT WE WERE
AFFLICTED ON EVERY SIDE: CONFLICTS
WITHOUT, FEARS WITHIN. BUT GOD,
WHO COMFORTS THE DEPRESSED, COMFORTED US
BY THE COMING OF TITUS.
2 Corinthians 7:5-6

7
Emotions:
The Volatile Variable

Emotions. Sometimes I wish I had a switch to turn them on or off. I used to think of myself as a very stable person—even-tempered, unemotional. But after raising four teenagers I seem to have caught their malady of roller-coaster emotions.

I love those feelings of joy and warmth that come with special events—the accomplishments of our children, a task well done, a marriage, a graduation, a spiritual victory. But I dread those down times of disappointment, troubling thoughts, failures, or anxiety. Yet both the up times and the down times are real.

In my devotional time I like to read things that stir my spiritual emotions, my feelings for God, for holiness, for love, for renewal. I long for the *feeling* of spirituality. I like to come off the mountain top with a spiritual glow. But what if those feelings are absent or fleeting? Where does the reality of lordship fit with my feelings?

We always live in the dynamic tension of fact and feelings. Certainly we want the warm sensation of close fellowship with God and others. We love the sense of closeness to God and the stirrings of spiritual response in our inner person. But we cannot demand them. The sweetness of that close communion with Christ is perhaps most clearly sensed in stark relief against the times of struggle and turmoil.

In fact, the visible and emotional battle in tribulation and trial may indicate more surely the reality of living under Christ's lordship. In his book on authority, Howard Butt writes, "We live in a sensual world; we face no bigger trap than religious sensuality. If we have an ecstatic experience with Christ we are tempted to feel he is in the ecstatic experience rather than that he is in all our experiences. He is in your ordinary routine just as he is in your mystical ecstasies: he is the down-to-earth God. Do not wait for goose bumps to reassure you that God is near. Thank him that he is near regardless of how you feel. Goose bumps are acceptable if you get them, but they really don't matter; life cannot continue a 24-hour-a-day-7-day-a-week-52-week-a-year-on-and-on-forever-goose-bump. It would deny your humanity. You are flesh, not glass. . . . Mystical sensations can be either of the Holy Spirit or of human nature, either of God or of Satan. Lots of Christians get mixed up worshiping their experiences: the idol of Christ plus their religious experiences. Thank God he is with you when the goose bumps go. Beware of spiritual lust. You are learning to live by raw faith."[1]

Emotions should not control us; we should control them. God certainly did not play a celestial joke on us when He gave us emotions. The lordship of Christ reigns in, through, and above our emotions.

This brings us to Paul's puzzling phrase: "as sorrowful yet always rejoicing" (2 Corinthians 6:10). Such opposite emotions—sorrow and joy. Can they coexist? Only for a Christian. "Sorrowful" describes Paul's condition at the time of writing—a product of his circumstances. "Always rejoicing" reflects a decision of his mind—a determined constant of Paul's life. He chose to rejoice, regardless of his circumstances.

In each emotion we can respond to the lordship of Christ. Jesus Himself set the pace. He wept over Jerusalem. He was a Man of sorrows and acquainted with grief. He sweat drops of blood in Gethsemane. In anger He overturned the money-changer's tables. He suffered the cross. To be like Him is to share in His sufferings and to be conformed to His death. Why should we expect less?

King David was a man of great emotions. The psalms reflect his pleas for deliverance from enemies, his sorrow over sin, his confession in tears, his rejoicing in song, his fear in defeat, and his joy in restoration. David learned to trust God in those times of stress. How should we respond?

In *sorrow* we can find our sustenance in God alone. Only He is sufficient for times of death and separation. "The Lord is near to the brokenhearted, and saves those who are crushed in spirit" (Psalm 34:18).

In *disappointment* and *despair* we turn to God for encouragement, as the psalmist did in Psalm 73:21-24.

When my heart was embittered, and I was pierced within, then I was senseless and ignorant; I was like a beast before Thee. Nevertheless I am continually with Thee; Thou hast taken hold of my right hand. With Thy counsel Thou wilt guide me, and afterward receive me to glory.

God understands our emotional pits and meets us at our point of need. We can respond to Christ's invitation: "Come to Me, all who are weary and heavy-laden, and I will give you rest" (Matthew 11:28). We sense our dependence on Christ when we are in distress even more than when everything in life goes smoothly.

In *fear* we always see our inadequacy. We realize that only God is our protection. Through Isaiah God promised: "Do not fear, for I am with you; do not look anxiously about you, for I am your God. I will strengthen you, surely I will help you, surely I will uphold you with My righteous right hand" (Isaiah 41:10).

Paul experienced fear.

> For even when we came into Macedonia our flesh had no rest, but we were afflicted on every side: conflicts without, fears within. But God, who comforts the depressed, comforted us by the coming of Titus.
> (2 Corinthians 7:5-6)

When we fear, we lose our self-confidence, and we acknowledge our dependence on God and on others.

Another kind of *sorrow* is that which results from sin. When we see our sin, we sorrow and seek repentance. The sorrow that follows an angry outburst, an infidelity, a dishonest act, or a lie can lead us to a more tender walk with God. "For the sorrow that is according to the will of God produces a repentance without regret, leading to salvation" (2 Corinthians 7:10).

None of these emotions is pleasant. They all hurt. Yet each one can lead to a deeper commitment to Christ's lordship.

Good feelings and emotions do not produce the same deep character responses. One whose life has always been a bed of roses (without the thorns) seldom has true spiritual depth. Yet joy also can be used to sharpen our walk with Christ. In happy times we can give praise with the fruit of our lips.

And Thy godly ones shall bless Thee. They shall speak
of the glory of Thy kingdom, and talk of Thy power;
to make known to the sons of men Thy mighty acts and
the glory and majesty of Thy kingdom. (Psalm 145:10-12)

We are happy when something pleasant or good happens
to us. Under the lordship of Christ, we give thanks to Him.
Success, rewards, and accolades must all be turned back to
God, because He is the source of all good things.

Do emotions, then, demonstrate whether or not we are
living under the lordship of Christ? In a sense yes—but not
so much the emotions themselves, but the response to Christ
that we make as a result of our emotions.

By themselves emotions are not reliable indicators of our
walk with God. They are but one indicator. Our feeling of
closeness to God should be compared with the reality of our
walk with Him. Constant seeking for religious experiences
reflects a wrong goal. We are to seek "the Kingdom of God
and His righteousness" and leave the emotional response to
God. In this way we surrender our emotions to His lordship.

I praise God for the warm, spiritual feelings I experience,
privately or in fellowship with other believers. God is kind
to give us those experiences. I also praise God for the emotions
that cause me distress, because then I sense much more my
dependence on God, and I seek Him more diligently.

NOTE:
  1. Howard Butt, *The Velvet Covered Brick* (New York: Harper & Row, 1973),
     page 108.

NEITHER DO I CONDEMN YOU;
GO YOUR WAY. FROM NOW ON SIN NO MORE.
John 8:11

8
Sin and Guilt:
The Freedom of Lordship

The woman's mind raced with panic as she saw the hatred in her accusers' eyes. Already stones were gripped in white-knuckled hands. Spittle filled their cheeks. The woman knew all too well the fate that was surely hers.

"Wait!" said the leader dressed in the stately robes. "I have an idea. Don't stone her now." The tight group of judges gathered for this trial puzzled over his delay. "That rascal called Jesus is in town," the leader continued. "Let's trap Him. Let's make Him see that He must keep the law."

"But why delay?" someone objected. "We caught her in the very act. Let's get it over with."

But the leader prevailed.

The woman's heart pounded with fear. She thought back

46

on the incident in which the man had been so convincing. This had not been her first act of adultery, yet she thought, "I'm not a real prostitute. I just do what these men tell me. After all, they should know the law. They were always men of prominence. They promised to protect me." But where was the man? He was as guilty as she, but they just let him go. What kind of justice was this? And why the delay of several hours?

Suddenly her accusers pushed her roughly through a crowd surrounding this Man she had never seen. The leader of her accusers rudely interrupted the Teacher who sat at the center of the crowd. "Teacher, this woman has been caught in adultery, in the very act" (John 8:4).

The Teacher turned His head slowly to the accuser. He said nothing, but gave him a piercing look.

The accuser hesitated, then blurted out, "Now in the Law Moses commanded us to stone such women; what then do You say?" (John 8:5).

The woman trembled. The crowd fell silent. Her accusers, all Pharisees and scribes, smirked. It was clearly a trick question. If Jesus condemned her, He could invite the hatred of the common people, who had little time for the crafty Pharisees. He might also incur the wrath of Roman law, which did not permit the Jews to make such judgments. Then the Teacher, known as Jesus, would appear to be a leader of an insurrection. Not to condemn her would seem to place Jesus against the Law of Moses. But there existed another point of law. Leviticus 20:10 clearly indicated that *both* the man and woman were to be stoned. If they had been "caught in the act," where was the man?

Jesus made no reply to His enemy's question, but simply stooped down and wrote on the ground with His finger. Perhaps He wrote the words of Leviticus 20:10, asking where the guilty man was.

The accusers ignored that and waited for an answer. Finally

Jesus straightened up and looked them in the eye, one by one. Then He said, "He who is without sin among you, let him be the first to throw a stone at her" (John 8:7). Then he stooped down and again wrote on the ground. He may have written the accusers' names and a recent sin:

Simeon—cheated his customers daily.
Jonas—committed adultery three weeks ago.
Jacob—falsely testified against a rival.

One by one the accusers silently slipped away. No one spoke another word.

Jesus again straightened up and found them all gone. The woman still stood there with her head bowed, legs trembling, and tears of fear running down her face. Yet she also felt a new sense of security in this Man whose name she did not know.

Jesus said kindly, "Woman, where are they? Did no one condemn you?"

"No one, Lord," she replied. What more could she say, for she was certainly guilty. She could run, but she seemed obligated to stand before this Man of unusual power and authority.

Jesus, again speaking kindly, said, "Neither do I condemn you; go your way. From now on sin no more" (John 8:11).

That Jesus considered her adultery was abundantly clear. That He forgave her sin was also clear. He did not just say, "I forgive you," but the more powerful declaration, "I do not condemn you." No condemnation—even though she was guilty.

Perhaps only those who have committed sexual sin can know the lingering feelings of guilt and remorse as their minds constantly relive the past. Even the new birth in Christ at times seems an inadequate comfort. And many other sins also plague our memories, lingering though forgiven.

Is Jesus Christ truly Lord over our past sin and our guilt? A glib, "Of course," and a few well chosen verses of Scripture do little to quench the fire of guilt feelings that rages through our consciousness. We must look deeper into the Scripture, the mind of God, and our inexplicable feelings.

Guilt is both the *human dilemma* and the *divine thorn*. Whatever its cause or source, guilt is painfully real. There is no dodging its presence. It springs up at the most unlikely time to ruin an hour of peace. Then it just as mysteriously recedes for a period of time. The *feeling* of guilt has little to do with whether or not we *are* guilty.

What is guilt? It is being responsible for an action or thought that was wrong—breaking a human rule or God's law. A person is guilty when he has broken a law. He *feels* guilty when he *both* believes that he has broken a law *and* is sorry that he did it. A person may believe that he is guilty but not be sorry—and thus have no *feeling* of guilt. Likewise a person may believe he is guilty when he is not, and still feel sorry and guilty. Actual guilt and false guilt are two different things.

So, there is *real guilt* and *false guilt*. Real guilt deserves a guilty feeling. False guilt deserves no feeling of guilt.

Let's consider the place of guilt in the nonChristian.

Every person in the world possesses a sense of some law for conduct.

> For when Gentiles who do not have the Law do instinctively the things of the Law, these, not having the Law, are a law to themselves, in that they show the work of the Law written in their hearts, their conscience bearing witness, and their thoughts alternately accusing or else defending them. (Romans 2:14-15)

Therefore all are guilty—whether or not they feel guilt or remorse. Sin separates them from God—all sin: pride, gossip, adultery, lying, stealing, etc.

But when a person comes to know Christ, *all* sin is forgiven.

"There is therefore now no condemnation for those who are in Christ Jesus" (Romans 8:1). That means a Christian no longer bears any guilt. As far as God is concerned, the sins never happened; they do not exist.

But were the sins committed? Yes. Do we remember them? Yes. Do they affect us today? Yes, but only to the extent that we allow them to affect us. Is there regret? Yes, the mind and memory frequently recall the sins back. But how should we respond? By feeling guilty? No! Rather, be thankful that God forgives the sin and that He has delivered us from its eternal consequences. Satan loves to keep us feeling guilty to prevent us from growing spiritually and to keep us from *experiencing* total forgiveness, which is an accomplished fact.

How, then, should we respond to those waves of guilt feelings? I suggest that we say, "I am not guilty, but I do *regret* what I did. I cannot change the past, but I can protect the future." Easy to say, but difficult to practice.

Satan is the source of the lie that says we are still guilty, even though we have been forgiven by God. When Satan confronted Jesus in the wilderness, Jesus rebuked him with the Scriptures. "It is written," Jesus said (Matthew 4:4). To counter Satan's attack of guilt feelings, memorize a few key Scripture verses to quote such as Romans 8:1,31 and 1 John 1:9.

The battle will often seem desperate. We know we are forgiven, and we can even quote the right Bible verses, but we still experience great swings of emotion. This will change as we grow in spiritual depth. As we increase our understanding of God's *grace*, we will experience greater release from guilt feelings. Grace is God's unmerited favor. We did not earn it; it is given freely. His grace covers all our sin. As we probe the depths of His redemptive grace in Christ Jesus our Lord, we will experience God the Father's love in a way that makes guilt only a shadow of the past. The lordship of Christ extends over our sin, our guilt, and our past. We can learn to live under that lordship, and not under the guilt for which the Lord died on the cross. Then we can sing with John Kent:

> Sovereign grace over sin abounding,
>   Ransomed souls, the tidings swell;
> 'Tis a deep that knows no sounding,
>   Who its breadth or length can tell?
> On its glories, on its glories
>   Let my soul forever dwell.
>
> What from Christ the soul can sever,
>   Bound by everlasting bands?
> Once in Him, in Him for ever,
>   Thus the eternal covenant stands.
> None shall pluck thee, none shall pluck thee
>   From the Strength of Israel's hands.

But what of the Christian who sins? Should he feel more guilty, having known our Lord and having power to keep from sin? He, too, comes to Christ to confess his sin and receive full, unquestioned forgiveness. But the confession is more than mere words repeated in rote fashion. It demands the confession of the heart, which is truly sorry for the sin. Glib naming or ritual reciting of one's sins does not meet the sense of 1 John 1:9, "If we confess our sins, He is faithful and righteous to forgive us our sins and to cleanse us from all unrighteousness." For a believer, this "cleansing from all un-righteousness" does not refer to salvation, but to fellowship with the Lord.

The Lord Jesus has authority to forgive sin, as He did for the woman caught in adultery. To us, too, He says, "Neither do I condemn you; go your way. From now on sin no more."

That miracle of true forgiveness overcomes all of our feelings of guilt.

9
Anxiety:
The Tensions of Lordship

Our daughter Kathy drove up to our house for a jogging rendezvous with her mother. She found the house surrounded by two fire trucks, an emergency medical vehicle, and an ambulance. She was certain that her mother had suffered a heart attack.

Our neighbor across the street saw the same scene and was sure I had a heart attack.

Both were wrong. Our daughter Karen had fainted suddenly while fixing her hair before going to work. She was gasping for breath and appeared to be having convulsions, so my wife called the emergency number. The firemen were there in two minutes. My wife rushed to the hospital following the ambulance, not knowing what had caused the problem.

52

Fifteen hundred miles away, I received word of the incident from the hospital emergency room, but with no answers and no prognosis.

Anxiety—our family got a full dose that day. All turned out well. Dehydration and lack of food following dental surgery the previous day had apparently caused the problem.

Perhaps anxiety was warranted in this case, yet I can reflect on dozens of situations in which my worry or another person's worry not only failed to help, but was a direct affront to God, a failure to trust Him.

Our anxiety and worry may be one of the most difficult areas to submit to Christ's lordship. "Be anxious for nothing" (Philippians 4:6) can seem an impossible directive to the panic-stricken heart.

Is all anxiety sin? I think not. As I write this, friends are awaiting the outcome of tests that will reveal if a brain tumor has reactivated in the body of a loved one. Are they anxious? Certainly. Is that lack of trust? No, it is human, a true concern of love.

Even in pain one can at the same time be anxious and yet trust. In such a case, anxiety expresses itself more like sorrow. In Gethsemane, Jesus sweat drops of blood and prayed, "If it is possible, let this cup pass from Me; yet not as I will, but as Thou wilt" (Matthew 26:39). Was that anxiety? Was it fear? Was it lack of trust in the Father? No, it was reality. The cross loomed ahead. Death was sure, as was separation from the Father.

As we face the reality of human frailty, we do sorrow and experience a form of anxiety or pain. The test of lordship comes when we decide whether or not to accept God's will in the matter.

We offend the Lord when the anxiety crosses the line from concern to distrust, when the anxiety focuses on future events over which we have neither knowledge nor control. Healthy concern for a sick spouse, financial difficulties, or a rebellious son or daughter crosses the line to anxiety when we begin to blame God, to make deals with Him if He will solve the problem, or to live in a state of panic and preoccupation. We would be callous to be unconcerned, but we lack faith when we cannot leave the outcome to God. This is particularly true when we, as the saying goes, "borrow trouble." Worrying about things that *might* happen or that *could* happen disturbs our peace and betrays our trust in God.

I come from a family of accomplished worriers. My early days as a child were consumed with anxiety. This continued into my high-school years. I worried about grades, the unknown, college, new ventures, my future, success, and dozens of other matters. Only as I began to make lordship commitments in my spiritual life did worries begin to diminish, but even today I can slip into anxiety.

The root of anxiety is *fear*: fear of the future, fear of failure, fear of the unknown, fear of impending disaster. We desperately want peace, not fear, and peace is promised to those who live under Christ's lordship: "Peace I leave with you; My peace I give to you; not as the world gives, do I give to you. Let not your heart be troubled, nor let it be fearful" (John 14:27).

The foundation of this peace is that God watches over His children to protect them and give them peace even in the midst of storms. He promises, "I will never desert you, nor will I ever forsake you." Therefore we can confidently say, "The Lord is my helper, I will not be afraid. What shall man do to me?" (Hebrews 13:5-6).

No one can invade your life without God's permission, and His permission in difficult times will always be accompanied by power and peace. As a child with her father is fearless, so we will not fear when we know God is in control.

We experience this reality by placing ourselves under

Christ's lordship. But what can be done about anxiety and fear? How does one go about changing those debilitating emotions? Let me share what I have found to be useful suggestions.

Write out what troubles you and makes you anxious. Be specific. Describe your feelings and the relevant facts. Record your anxious thoughts and fears. Often in the stark reality of seeing anxiety in black and white, we gain a clearer perspective.

Then make a list of what you *can do or control* and what is totally *outside your control*. You *can* pray, talk to people, pay a debt, work harder, or gather information. You *cannot* control another person's actions, change the weather, redo history, control the future, or change the outcome of another individual's decisions. Only God can do those things.

In reflecting on these two lists, quietly and simply, acknowledge God's sovereignty in all events. Confess your sin when sin is involved. In prayer, declare your dependence on God either to change or prevent circumstances, and your willingness to live with His decision. Verbally place yourself under the lordship of Christ. You may need daily to give the circumstances of your anxiety over to God, asking for His peace. You will know when you experience a breakthrough of peace flooding your mind and body. It is like a cool shower on a hot day.

As God delivers you, issue by issue, from anxiety, take note of what He did for you. Then, when new issues arise—as they will—you can *remember* what God did. There is nothing like having experienced God's deliverance to gain confidence that He will again deliver. God commanded the wandering, errant children of Israel, "Remember all the way which the Lord your God has led you in the wilderness these forty years" (Deuteronomy 8:2). Remember—and take courage, like the hymn writer Paul Gerhardt:

> Put thou thy trust in God,
> In duty's path go on;

Walk in His strength with faith and hope,
    So shall thy work be done.

Give to the winds thy fears;
    Hope, and be undismayed:
God hears thy sighs and counts thy tears;
    God shall lift up thy head.

Commit thy ways to Him,
    Thy works into His hands,
And rest on His unchanging word,
    Who heaven and earth commands.

Though countless years go by,
    His covenant shall endure;
Though clouds and darkness hide His path,
    The promised grace is sure.

Through waves and clouds and storms
    His power will clear thy way:
Wait thou His time; the darkest night
    Shall end the brightest day.

Leave to His sovereign sway
    To choose and to command;
So shalt thou, wondering, own His way,
    How wise, how strong His hand.

Let us in life, in death,
    His steadfast truth declare,
And publish with our latest breath
    His love and guardian care.

THE LUST OF THE FLESH, AND
THE LUST OF THE EYES
AND THE BOASTFUL PRIDE OF LIFE,
IS NOT FROM THE FATHER.
1 John 2:16

10
Lust or Lordship?

Some men and women lust for sex. Some lust for food. Others, for comfort or possessions. Still others, for power. Each lust exerts its peculiar magnetic influence over the mind and body.

Everyone lusts for something. Everyone battles the irresistible urges of lust. Some win the battle. Others give in and suffer greatly.

Christians who deeply desire to walk in the lordship of Jesus Christ are particularly troubled when lust continues to plague their lives. We each seem to possess an "Achilles heel" in this matter of lust. Even the most mature Christian battles lust daily.

Is all desire lust? Certainly not. Where does legitimate longing and desire end and lust begin? No simple answer exists for this question. All of us must determine the limits in our own lives.

First, we need to define lust. Lust is an inordinate desire to gratify the senses of the body or mind which is so strong that we are under its control. In some translations of Scripture the word is translated "desire." Lust is desire in excess. It is the illegitimate extension of God-given human desires to selfish indulgence. It is losing control of natural human drives.

If we limit the concept of lust to sexual matters, we ignore its broader, insidious implications. Christians often conquer areas of sexual lust and then fall to more subtle inroads of lust. Sexual lust is more obvious, because it easily grows into sexual sin clearly forbidden in Scripture. The sinful results of other kinds of lust usually manifest themselves in areas of character or actions that are not as easily identified as sin, such as power grabbing, lack of discipline, selfishness.

Let us examine a few Greek words in the New Testament often translated as "lust."

• *epithumeo*—set heart upon, long for, covet, desire, lust (as in Matthew 5:28: "everyone who looks on a woman to lust for her has committed adultery with her already in his heart").

• *epithumetes*—a craver (as in 1 Corinthians 10:6: "we should not crave evil things").

• *epithumia*—a longing for what is forbidden (as in 1 Peter 2:11: "abstain from fleshly lusts, which wage war against the soul").

• *orexis*—excitement of the mind, longing after, lust (as in Romans 1:27: "men . . . burned in their desire [lust] towards one another").

• *hedone*—sensual delight, desire, lust, pleasure (as in James 4:1: "What is the source of quarrels and conflicts among you? Is not the source your pleasures [lusts] that wage war in your members?") *Hedone* can be recognized as the root word for hedonism—the focus on sensual pleasures that characterizes many cultures in our world today.

So much for analysis. What are we to do? 1 John 2:16 categorizes three lusts: "For all that is in the world, the lust of the flesh and the lust of the eyes and the boastful pride of life, is not from the Father, but is from the world." Lust of the flesh refers to that which the body craves—sex, food, ease. The lust of the eyes is a desire to possess what one sees—material possessions, a home, a car, clothing. The boastful pride of life is lust for position, power, and even an excessive desire for a healthy body or spiritual experience.

Consider several of these as they relate to your own life.

Food. We abuse our bodies with food—both in amount and kind. Watch people in public places and notice the U.S. number of significantly overweight people—almost fifty percent of the population. It's virtually the same—or worse—among Christians. The issue is one of lust and lack of control. Part of the problem is wrong foods and part is lust to eat.

Body worship. Lust for food has an opposite: the lust to be attractive, fashionable, and in good shape. We can worship our bodies and be preoccupied with health foods and physical fitness—a lust for the "body beautiful." We need to consider our motives. Do we wish to serve God better, to be more alert, and to exercise self-control? Or are we motivated by pride, arrogance, or compulsion?

Sex. God made us sexual beings with natural longings and desires. But He also placed boundaries on our sexual behavior. Sexual lust can pervade the mind of a married person as well as a single person. The balance of lust and love is discerned when one can keep thoughts and body pure, and when lustful thoughts do not permeate one's thinking. Sex always begins in the mind. We must guard what we allow to enter the mind. Sexual and immoral thoughts can be increased by coarse books, magazines, movies, and television. If you cannot control your mental and physical sexual lust, consider abstaining from these four media for several months and see if your lust decreases.

Lust always precedes action. Action brings overt sin. Let's attack the sin at its point of origin—lust.

Position. We all want to be known and respected by some group of people—family, church, coworkers, neighbors, friends. We can lust for position in a group. This is the "boastful pride of life," which deceives us into thinking that meaning resides in one's position. The inner human urge to compare oneself with others leads to ultimate disappointment. Even the most spiritual of believers can be drawn into this deception.

Under the lordship of Christ the only truly fulfilling position is that of servant. This was Paul's view. "What then is Apollos? And what is Paul? Servants through whom you believed" (1 Corinthians 3:5). "Paul and Timothy, bond-servants of Christ Jesus" (Philippians 1:1). When God, in His sovereignty, places us in a position of authority or respect, let us remember that such a position only provides the opportunity to serve.

Power. "Power corrupts, and absolute power corrupts absolutely," as Lord Acton said. Almost everyone wields power over some other person, but some individuals lust for power and control. It is an illegitimate desire, for the motive is wrong.

Powerful men fear wise men because a wise man can lead without power, but a powerful man leads only by power. Whether it be husband over wife, parent over child, teacher over pupils, employer over employee, pastor over people, or supervisor over workers, the temptation to misuse power always lurks in the mind.

God puts many people in a position of power and authority. Believers must not misuse this power, but place it under the lordship of Christ. Jesus' example and teaching set the pattern for people in power.

You know that the rulers of the Gentiles lord it over them, and their great men exercise authority over them. It is not so among you, but whoever wishes to become great among you shall be your servant . . . just as the Son of Man did not come to be served, but to serve, and to give His life a ransom for many. (Matthew 20:25-28)

Let us not lust for power—in the world or in the church.

Possessions. Who doesn't want a nicer home, better furniture, a newer car, nicer clothes, a more powerful stereo system, labor-saving gadgets? How easy it is to lust for possessions! Upward mobility is a natural instinct. Only a rare few choose to live more moderately than their means permit. The lust for things—one aspect of the lust of the eyes—can destroy one's spiritual hunger. By contrast, it was said of John Wesley that he was "a man who died leaving behind nothing but his Bible, his horse, and the Methodist Church."

Spiritual experience or power. We all want a greater desire for God and His Word. But can spiritual hunger become spiritual lust? I think it is possible. We can hunger so much after spiritual experiences that we forget that the source of all such experience is God Himself. I have seen people go into depression when they did not reach the level of feeling and experience with God that they longed for. We may desire the feeling of the experience rather than God Himself. He may take us through sorrow and trials before we ever experience the depth of His presence.

Inordinate spiritual lust can lead to doctrinal error and a seeking for the externals of spirituality while missing the reality. Simon of Acts 8 demonstrated such lust when he tried to buy spiritual power. Let us not fall into the same trap.

How can we avoid the excesses of these lusts and their subsequent spiritual damage? Paul gives us some insight.

For you were called to freedom, brethren; only do not turn your freedom into an opportunity for the flesh, but

through love serve one another . . . walk by the Spirit,
and you will not carry out the desire [lust] of the flesh.
For the flesh sets its desire against the Spirit, and the
Spirit against the flesh; for these are in opposition to one
another, so that you may not do the things that you please.
(Galatians 5:13,16-17)

The power to control lust resides in the Holy Spirit's
control of the believer's life. The Spirit-controlled life is the
only answer. The Spirit leads us to a life submitted to the lordship of Christ.

Lest there be any question as to what he meant, Paul goes
on to describe the deeds of the flesh.

Now the deeds of the flesh are evident, which are:
immorality, impurity, sensuality, idolatry, sorcery,
enmities, strife, jealousy, outbursts of anger, disputes,
dissensions, factions, envyings, drunkenness, carousings,
and things like these, of which I forewarn you just as I
have forewarned you that those who practice such things
shall not inherit the kingdom of God. (Galatians 5:19-21)

We must not allow our lusts to lead us to these sins.

What lusts and desires plague you? Allow the lordship of
Christ to excise them. The remedy is given in Romans 13:14:
"But put on the Lord Jesus Christ, and make no provision for
the flesh in regard to its lusts." Put on Jesus Christ as Lord.
In that surrender lies victory.

LORD, IF YOU HAD BEEN HERE,
MY BROTHER WOULD NOT HAVE DIED.
John 11:21

11
Disappointment: The Trauma of Unmet Expectations

Jesus came too late. Lazarus was already dead. Though Jesus knew of his illness, He chose to come late. While Mary and Martha grieved for their brother, they expressed disappointment that Jesus had not come when they called for him: "If you had been here . . ." (John 11:21).

How many times in life have we been disappointed, thinking "If only God had . . ."? But God hadn't, and we were disappointed. From the disappointment of not going to the circus as a child to the news of being turned down for a job, we have learned to tolerate disappointment, submerge it, and go on with life. But each disappointment hurts and leaves its impression on our emotional lives. Some disappointments leave deep, long-term impressions on us. They are not easily passed off and forgotten. They lead to deeper complications and responses.

Our daughter Karen seemed to experience more than her share. While in high school, she set her heart on being accepted into an outstanding singing group. Finally, she was accepted. Life was great for her. Then, we found that the leaders were teaching religious doctrine that we felt was wrong. I met with the leaders to see if Karen could sing in the group without attending the Bible studies. They refused. We asked Karen to leave the group. There were tears and deep disappointment. To her credit, though she did not fully understand the doctrinal issues, she agreed, in spite of the hurt. Our hearts went out to her, knowing how bad she felt.

Recently, at age 22, Karen applied to another Christian singing group in Europe with only two openings for sopranos. After the deadline we daily watched the mailbox. Finally a letter came. Several members of our family were sitting in our living room, anxiously waiting as she opened the letter. There was a long silence, then she read part of it, clearly a form letter of rejection. More disappointment. All her plans for the next year were now up in the air. Again, to our great admiration, she took it well. But I wondered why God didn't let her experience this desire of her heart. Her disappointment hurt all of us.

In His graciousness God did not allow the story to end there. Stripped of her plans, Karen began to get involved in our church's college youth group. There she met the youth pastor, and a relationship began to deepen. Ten months later they were married, fulfilling one of her dreams—to be the wife of a pastor. God's timing was perfect. The process developed Karen's character in a way that success never could.

Unfortunately, disappointments are not always resolved like that. Disappointment often turns to discouragement. Discouragement can be the consequence of a series of disappointments, until we begin to lose hope. Then discouragement can turn into despair, and we see no hope at all for life issues turning out well. Finally, despair turns to deep depression, which affects our emotional well-being.

Disappointment, discouragement, despair, depression—a tragic chain of emotional events. What can we do to prevent this sequence? The answer lies in the way we handle ordinary disappointment.

How we handle disappointment centers around our biblical view of hope.

> Therefore having been justified by faith, we have peace
> with God through our Lord Jesus Christ . . . and we
> exult in hope of the glory of God. And not only this,
> but we also exult in our tribulations, knowing that
> tribulation brings about perseverance; and perseverance,
> proven character; and proven character, hope; and
> hope does not disappoint, because the love of God has
> been poured out within our hearts through the Holy Spirit
> who was given to us. (Romans 5:1-5)

We all live by hope. Disappointment occurs when hopes are not fulfilled, and in particular when we hope for the wrong things. We become disappointed when events do not turn out as we want or expect. Then our picture of the future is shattered. We wrestle with our own view of what is best for us compared to God's view of our best.

When we live under the control of the flesh, our hopes are bound up in a temporal system of values and expectations. When we live under the lordship of Christ, our hopes are surrendered to Him.

Practically, how does hope daily convert disappointment into joy?

The ultimate hope centers around the promised return

of Jesus Christ and the resurrection of the body. Paul speaks of "looking for the blessed hope and the appearing of the glory of our great God and Savior, Christ Jesus" (Titus 2:13), and of "the hope of eternal life, which God, who cannot lie, promised long ages ago" (Titus 1:2). Paul declares, "If we have hoped in Christ in this life only, we are of all men most to be pitied" (1 Corinthians 15:19). Such hope carries an eternal dimension that overshadows the uncertainty of life's daily events. The certainty of this hope depends only on the trustworthiness of God, not the feelings of the moment.

Biblical hope is unlike our weak use of the word in everyday language: "I hope I can pass that exam," or "I hope I will get well." That weak hope is little more than a wish or an empty desire. We hope in certainty. In the Old Testament the word implied to "look ahead eagerly with confident expectation."[1]

That reflects the psalmist's bold assertion, "For I hope in Thee, O Lord; Thou wilt answer, O Lord my God" (Psalm 38:15). Hope is God's certainty, not our weak wish.

Our hope is in God—His Word, His character, His name, and His promise. God spoke, and He will do it. Such hope rests in the solid work of Christ and the written Word of God. We do not find hope in our feelings, but in our knowledge of the revealed God incarnate, Jesus the Christ.

From Adam to the Revelation given to John, God recorded the evidence of His love and promises, and by them we live and hope. When we neglect His Word, we lose sight of our hope. Day by day our hope is built up as we feed on His Word. Like Jeremiah we can say, "Thy words were found and I ate them, and Thy words became for me a joy and the delight of my heart" (Jeremiah 15:16). Not discouragement, but joy, delight—and hope.

Hope that overpowers disappointment believes that God always works for our best in every circumstance. Paul understood this, even in prison.

Now I want you to know, brethren, that my circumstances
have turned out for the greater progress of the gospel.... For
I know that this shall turn out for my deliverance ...
according to my earnest expectation and hope, that I
shall not be put to shame in anything, but that with
all boldness, Christ shall even now, as always, be
exalted in my body, whether by life or by death.
(Philippians 1:12,19-20)

Hope convinces us that every event of life will be used
by God for our good. "God causes all things to work together
for good" (Romans 8:28). Just as God promised Israel regarding
their captivity in Babylon, so He promises us, "For I know the
plans that I have for you, . . . plans for welfare and not for
calamity to give you a future and a hope" (Jeremiah 29:11).

Hope gives strength from God. He commands, "Be strong,
and let your heart take courage, all you who hope in the Lord"
(Psalm 31:24). Courage is the strength to wait on God. In
both Old and New Testaments, hope carries the sense of waiting
on God. It is intrinsically bound in the "big three" of the
Christian life—faith, hope, and love. Faith believes God; hope
waits on God; love reveals God's character. Hebrews defines
faith in terms of hope: "Now faith is the assurance of things
hoped for, the conviction of things not seen" (Hebrews 11:1).

Finally, the roots of disappointment are severed in the
deep love relationship we have in Christ, this is the mystery
Paul gave his life to proclaim: "Christ in you, the hope of
glory" (Colossians 1:27). The living Christ, indwelling us and
guarding us, changes disappointment to hope and dread to
expectation. Under the authority of His lordship, life takes on
a new dimension of hope.

Does this mean that a believer will never experience
disappointment? No, but that disappointed feeling turns to
hope and joy as Jesus Christ ministers to our hearts with

the reality of His hope. This is not a magic formula which, taken by the teaspoonful twice daily, suddenly erases fleshly, human sorrow. It is, rather, a living, vital interaction daily with our Lord and a surrender to His loving care.

NOTE:
  1. Lawrence O. Richards, *Expository Dictionary of Bible Words* (Grand Rapids: Zondervan, 1985), page 343.

12
Attitude:
The Dilemma of
Motive and Mind

The "Attitude Adjustment Hour" sounds intriguing, but it is just a euphemism for the "happy hour"—cocktails after work at a local bar. Alcohol is just one of the many supposed antidotes for a crummy attitude. And it works—for a few hours. But soon, like any drug, it hooks the user and produces even more serious problems. The real problem lies hidden in the mind and heart.

Even for the Christian, attitudes seem almost uncontrollable. "Getting up on the wrong side of bed" is a code phrase for a bad attitude. We don't like it, but it is there. Or it lurks just under the surface of our temper, waiting to be triggered by a chance remark or irritating circumstance.

When our attitudes turn sour, we find it nearly impossible

to hide. I wish I could take back those cutting words, piercing stares, and rude actions that bubbled to the surface and hurt my children and wife. My excuse for a bad attitude that day rings hollow to those I have hurt, and I feel angry that I cannot control my mind and responses. Even when I gain control of my words and actions, my mind still harbors that bad attitude. Sometimes it is like a headache that stays all day. Like a headache, once started, it seems impossible to stop. In times like that I *know* I do not exhibit the "mind of Christ."

A bad attitude springs up from so many unexpected sources: a traffic jam, a long line at the store, expected mail that did not come, an interruption, an unkind comment, a bad night's sleep, a cold, a rainstorm on a day off, a scratch on a new car, a child's request to go to the store, and hundreds of other minor events.

Have you ever tried to light a campfire in the forest with wet or green wood and a match? The wood simply will not burn. The fuel must be ready to burn, or there will be no fire. Likewise, events cannot ignite a bad attitude unless the mind is ready to respond negatively.

What makes a bad attitude? We can identify several sources of our attitude: our personal history, background, frame of mind, way of thinking, or a decision of the will.

Our *personal history* deeply affects our attitude. Experiences from childhood to adulthood remain engraved in our memories and responses. We relate current events to past events and anticipate their results. A past pattern of anger or suspicion continues to emerge in our attitude today. Past failure or frustration leads to a pessimistic view of life. Past betrayals of friendship or disappointment with the opposite sex cause us to mistrust people. Our minds become a tape recording of the past, which can be erased only as Christ becomes Lord of our past.

Each of us comes from a particular *background* of home,

culture, prejudices, and habits. From birth, attitudes grow and take root in our lives. It is discouraging to see traits in your own life that you saw and disliked in your parents, but in the same way good, healthy, and godly attitudes can also be transmitted. We should recognize both. We can never escape our family and cultural heritage—with its good and bad traits. We surrender this background to the lordship of Christ, knowing His sovereignty in both birth and background. Background is never an excuse for ungodly attitudes or behavior, but only an explanation of the source.

In the present, attitude is both *a frame of mind* and *a way of thinking*. Paul said,

> You were taught, with regard to your former way of life, to put off your old self, which is being corrupted by its deceitful desires; to be made new in the attitude of your minds; and to put on the new self, created to be like God in true righteousness and holiness. (Ephesians 4:22-24, NIV)

In Christ we are to be made new in our attitude. The attitude and the mind are intricately intertwined. How we think determines our attitude. Thinking badly of someone forms a negative attitude about them. We can choose how we think—especially in Christ. The Greek word used here (*phroneo*) means to think or to form an opinion or judgment. It "leads us through the process of evaluating a situation and, on the basis of our evaluation, adopting an attitude or disposition to act."[1]

We should think in a way that reflects the lordship and servant spirit of the Lord Jesus Christ. He gave Himself. He saw our sin and still had compassion. He knew our inner hearts and still loved us. He saw the deviousness of our minds and still reached out to us. Can we do less? Can we not overlook the foibles and faults of others and build an attitude of love? "Have this attitude in yourselves which was also in Christ Jesus" (Philippians 2:5). Paul goes on to say that Jesus "emptied Himself" and "humbled Himself." Christ is our pattern.

Finally, a right attitude involves a *decision of the will.* We can decide what and how to think about people and situations. When feelings and prejudices of the past erupt in our minds and emotions, we can evaluate their validity. We test them by the Scripture and the example of Jesus Christ.

Paul said, "Set your mind on the things above, not on the things that are on earth" (Colossians 3:2). Obviously, Paul thought that a Christian could choose to set his mind on one thing or another. Without subscribing to a philosophy of "positive thinking" from a psychological viewpoint, there is much to be said for a positive frame of mind or attitude. Have you ever observed the response of two people to the same set of circumstances? One sees every negative aspect and casts a shadow of gloom. The other sees the positive things and radiates a sense of optimism. We choose whether to look on the positive or negative side of events and people. How we choose determines our attitude.

No one enjoys the company of a negative person. They chase away friends—in fact, they destroy them. Think of those kinds of attitudes—a critical attitude, a judgmental attitude, a nit-picking attitude, a doubting attitude, a cynical attitude, a sour attitude, a resentful attitude, an angry attitude, a haughty attitude, a superior attitude, a snobbish attitude, a selfish attitude. All of these are attitudes unsurrendered to the lordship of Christ. They do not look for the person's good, think well of them, give encouragement, or build them up. Fundamentally, they are attitudes of inward-looking and self-centered people. They focus on self, not others. They lack the character trait of humility found in a true disciple of Jesus Christ. That is why Paul urges,

Whatever is true, whatever is honorable, whatever is right, whatever is pure, whatever is lovely, whatever is of good repute, if there is any excellence and if anything worthy of praise, let your mind dwell on these things. (Philippians 4:8)

"Let your mind dwell," "set your mind"—both actions of the will. We *choose* to have a good attitude.

I am not advocating an escape from reality, but rather a godly and positive attitude toward it. Sadness, anger, sorrow, and hurt may all enter our lives and emotions, but they do not need to remain. We deal with them under the lordship of Christ. We choose our responses and attitudes.

The deepest desire of God's heart is to change our character to Christlikeness. Our attitude reveals our true character. It is the evidence of Christlikeness.

We can no longer give the excuse, "That's just the way I am. I can't change." Paul declared, "If any man is in Christ, he is a new creature; the old things passed away; behold, new things have come" (2 Corinthians 5:17). As new creations in Christ we can change. God gives us the power to change as we surrender our lives, minds, and wills to Him. We do that by praying, "God, take these ingrained attitudes of my mind and radically transform them through the power of Your Holy Spirit into the likeness of Your Son, Jesus Christ."

NOTE:
1. Richards, *Expository Dictionary*, page 86.

LORD OF MY TIME AND POSSESSIONS

FOR WHERE YOUR TREASURE IS,
THERE WILL YOUR HEART BE ALSO.
Luke 12:34

13
True Treasures:
A Lordship Value System

Possessions cast a strange spell over people. When I was a young Air Force officer, my wife and I owned a modest amount of furniture and personal effects. But one thing had to be first-class: my stereo high-fidelity system. I wanted the best and had at least a start toward building a good system. Early one Saturday morning I had gone out for an appointment. When I returned, the house was quiet except for my two-year-old son, Steve. He was happily tramping around the living room—on my hi-fi records!

I recall now with embarrassment and regret the angry words I expressed. Little Steve didn't know what was wrong. But at that moment I valued the records more than I valued my relationship with Steve. My value system was confused.

A few months later we moved from Florida to Ohio to return to graduate school. Our household goods were shipped and stored in a warehouse until we would arrive after a month of holiday. We selected an apartment and called for our household goods, only to find that everything we owned had been destroyed in a warehouse fire: wedding pictures, furniture, clothing, mementos—and my stereo system! Nothing left except what had traveled with us in our little Volkswagen bug! Strangely enough, I felt calm. I experienced no sorrow—only a sense of freedom from those possessions. Perhaps I was getting too attached to things. God knew I needed my toys wrenched out of my hands.

Where is your heart these days? What treasure consumes your thinking? It is so easy to tie our hearts to material things. All of us seem to have a love affair with the world, even though we grow spiritually. Jesus reveals His thinking on material possessions in these perceptive statements:

> Do not be anxious for your life, as to what you shall
> eat; nor for your body, as to what you shall put on. For
> life is more than food, and the body than clothing. . . .
> And do not seek what you shall eat, and what you shall
> drink, and do not keep worrying . . . your Father knows that
> you need these things. But seek for His kingdom, and
> these things shall be added to you. . . . Sell your
> possessions and give to charity; make yourselves purses
> which do not wear out, an unfailing treasure in heaven,
> where no thief comes near, nor moth destroys. For where
> your treasure is, there will your heart be also.
> (Luke 12:22-34)

Living under the lordship of Christ means coming to terms with attachment to our possessions. We learn to hold them loosely, to give, to share. Christ teaches us to guard our hearts from valuing the wrong treasures.

We seem to go through the stage of setting our affections on things without eternal value. In themselves, these things are not bad. But as they consume and control our thinking, they become spoiled.

In our younger years, we look for education, marriage, a good job, and financial freedom. We buy cars, furniture, and amusements. In a few years we begin seeking status, more money, our own house, nicer clothes, and more comforts. In our forties we transfer attention to our children's accomplishments, ease and recreation, increased financial freedom, perhaps a bigger house, and extra comforts. The issue of future security in retirement drives us in new directions. This is the American middle-class dream. What is wrong with it? The problem lies with a self-centered focus on the material.

What does it take to break this love affair with material things? How does God get our attention? Sometimes it happens through the death of someone near us or a sudden health problem. Then we begin to see life as it really is and understand Christ's teaching, "Beware, and be on your guard against every form of greed; for not even when one has an abundance does his life consist of his possessions" (Luke 12:15).

It usually takes a shock to our system to wake us up. Only when we see friends, relationships, or health slipping away do we see the futility of possessions—passing things that clutter and complicate our lives. Real life is more than possessions, power, or success. It is being fully in tune with the lordship of Christ, which gives us ultimate perspective on our possessions. We may then keep them or give them; it doesn't really matter. They are temporary, they have no ultimate worth.

There are people who would give all of their riches for a good marriage, a restored relationship with a son or daughter, or a healthy body. But why do we wait for the touch of disaster to get our attention? Can we not take God at His Word and change our value system? Can we not change and seek His Kingdom first?

Yes. We can. And we will as we surrender to His lordship day by day. The poorest of men can be rich in God, the richest of men can be spiritual paupers. Choose to be rich toward God, and He can choose to give you much or little. In that much or little you will find your every need met.

THEREFORE DO NOT WORRY ABOUT TOMORROW,
FOR TOMORROW WILL WORRY ABOUT ITSELF.
EACH DAY HAS ENOUGH TROUBLE OF ITS OWN.
Matthew 6:34 (NIV)

COME NOW, YOU WHO SAY, "TODAY OR
TOMORROW, WE SHALL GO TO SUCH AND SUCH
A CITY, AND SPEND A YEAR THERE AND
ENGAGE IN BUSINESS AND MAKE A PROFIT."
YET YOU DO NOT KNOW WHAT YOUR LIFE WILL
BE LIKE TOMORROW.
James 4:13-14

14
The Future:
Is God in Control?

In industry, in education, in government, in Christian organizations, and in church planning, strategy for the future
dominates the thinking of leaders. Survival in business demands it. Strategic planning has become the bread and butter
of the business consultant.

The future holds both fascination and fear. Fascination is
the curiosity of wanting to know, and fear is the apprehension
of disappointment and hurt. In past centuries mystics, fortune-
tellers, and soothsayers sold their predictive services—with
no guarantees, of course. Even in this advanced technological
age, the most reputable of magazines and newspapers carry
the predictions of popular psychics with no hint of ridicule
or question. We are little different from people of primitive

times, because we, too, look for knowledge of the future.

Christians possess the same curiosity, fascination, and fear. But what do the contrasting verses heading this chapter mean? On one hand, we are told to not be concerned about the future, and on the other hand, to think ahead and prepare for the future.

Christians through the years have lived on both sides of the issue. Some decry planning and providing for the future on the grounds that such actions deny living by faith. For that reason, some believers refuse to buy insurance, set aside savings, or prepare for difficult circumstances of the future. After all, if Christ is Lord, will He not provide?

Some years ago a friend of mine subscribed to this belief and so did not buy auto insurance. Then, as "luck" would have it, he had an accident. He did not have enough money to pay the bills. Someone gave him the money to pay his debt. A mature believer asked, "Aren't you glad Frank didn't have as much faith as you did, so he could pay your bills?"

At the other extreme, we find believers who plan meticulously, load up with great amounts of insurance, save up large amounts of money, and make retirement planning an obsession. They do nothing without a careful plan and an assured outcome. In church and Christian organizations, they insist on operating just as they would in a business. To them faith is only a Christian buzzword used as an excuse for sloppy planning.

Perhaps you, like I, squirm uncomfortably at both of these approaches. Both possess some truth, but life at extremes seldom works.

In the Bible we discover two constructive and complimentary truths regarding the future.

1. We are not to be anxious and worried about the future, because it is totally in God's hands. He will provide for us in every area of life.

2. We are to plan and make decisions in light of the future. This includes providing for our own needs and the needs of our families, our spiritual growth, and the well-being of the Body of Christ and our community.

We face the lordship of Christ in the challenge to believe that God will provide *and* that God will bless our conscientious decisions.

I know about anxiety. My early life—childhood, teens, and young adulthood—was often plagued with worry and anxiety. Almost always the anxiety was connected with the future. My active mind raced ahead to possibilities of disaster and calamity. Would the class bully pester me again? Would I find my way around at the new school? Would I have friends? Would I pass the test? Would I run out of money and have to quit college? Could I understand a certain subject?

My nights were spent in sleeplessness with knots of anxiety in my stomach. I knew that panic-filled sensation of worry. Only as I grew spiritually in Christ did these dreaded feelings come under the lordship of Christ, who promised, "Peace I leave with you; My peace I give to you; not as the world gives, do I give to you. Let not your heart be troubled, nor let it be fearful" (John 14:27). Christ's peace does not come to us only by our repeating this promise over and over. Peace comes as we learn to abide in Christ through obedience and faith.

The book of Proverbs encourages us to plan. "The prudent man considers his steps. A wise man is cautious and turns away from evil, but a fool is arrogant and careless" (Proverbs 14:15-16). "Prepare plans by consultation, and make war by wise guidance" (Proverbs 20:18). Of course, the plan we want is God's plan. Planning in a biblical manner involves searching the Scriptures for principles and commands, praying, and then stepping out on faith. Proverbs 16:9 shows the relationship between our plans and God's plans: "The mind of man plans his way, but the Lord directs his steps." Every human plan should be subjected to the lordship of Christ as He directs step by step. In making our plans we must understand that God has a plan for us and His plan is good. Our plan and His plan coincide as we obey His Word on a day-to-day basis.

As we surrender to the lordship of Christ regarding the future, one word stands out—hope. Our hope is the ultimate return of Christ and eternal life with Him. The future revolves around this hope. It places all of our plans in perspective. Someone once said, "Plan as though you would live forever, and live as though Christ would return tomorrow."

As we seek God's plan for our future, we seek to avoid two errors. The first is *superstition*. Who of us has not lived more carefully, prayed more fervently, and practiced spiritual exercises more faithfully when some important issue of life is about to be decided? A test, a job opportunity, a raise, the sale of a home, a promotion—each can lead us to act as superstitiously as someone avoiding a black cat, walking under a ladder, or throwing salt over his shoulder. God sees the heart, not just the few days of good behavior. What He wants is a true yielding to the lordship of Christ.

The second, and opposite, error is *fatalism*. This view states that nothing I do or think can influence the future. What will be will be. This denies the dynamic relationship between man and God. He does respond to prayer and to the yielding of our lives.

Inventor Charles F. Kettering said, "My concern is with the future, for I will live the rest of my life there."[1] And so will we. When our lives are surrendered to the lordship of Christ, our thoughts of the future will be free of anxiety and worry; our plans will be made in confidence and faith.

NOTE:
1. Charles F. Kettering, *Companion* (September 1977), page 4.

MY TIMES ARE IN THY HAND.
Psalm 31:15

15
Time:
The Unrenewable Resource

Time respects no one and waits for no one. We each count the minutes, hours, or days with anticipation of a delicious event. It comes and passes in a moment, flashing into memory, often leaving a vacuum of emptiness. Not one of us knows the allotted quantity of time in life. We only know that each day we possess the same amount. We invest or spend it all.

Time governs every facet of our meager existence. Night and day, rest and activity, weeks and months, summer and winter, years and decades—all mark the cycles of every life.

In this boundary of time, our surrender to the lordship of Christ is tested daily. The test comes in the simple words *patience* and *waiting*.

Often the lordship of Christ is tested in the crucible of

waiting: waiting for a mate, waiting for maturity, waiting for answers to prayer, waiting to find a job, waiting for a rebellious son or daughter to repent, waiting for health to improve, waiting for relief from pressure, waiting for a conflict to end, waiting for improved finances, waiting for a baby to be conceived, waiting for tomorrow or next week or next year, waiting for suffering to end. Waiting patiently, without ulcers, without anger, with peace, with assurance—knowing only that God will work, but not how or when He will work.

God's list of heroes and heroines is filled with people who waited. King David waited in the cave of Adullam as he fled from Saul. Moses spent forty years in the desert before he returned to lead Israel out of Egypt and another forty years of wandering in the wilderness—and still brought the people only to the border of the Promised Land. Job waited for God as his health and all he held dear disappeared before his eyes. Elizabeth and Zacharias waited until old age to bear the special child, John the Baptist. Paul the apostle waited in prison, hoping for deliverance which never came, while he wrote letters that are now a part of the New Testament. God waited for the "fullness of time" to send Jesus to die for the sins of the world.

Waiting is part of God's plan in many circumstances of life.

I remember many times of impatience in waiting. Waiting—for high-school graduation, for college graduation, for my wedding day, for a check to come in the mail, for news of a new job, and for countless events, great and small. As I grew older, I controlled my impatience better. Yet the old feeling lay just below the surface of my mind—and it still does.

Time and *patience* are intricately related. Patience is waiting on God's timing. Patience is one of the fruits of the Spirit listed in Galatians 5:22-23. Isaiah said, "But they that wait upon the LORD shall renew their strength; they shall mount up with wings like eagles; they shall run, and not be weary;

and they shall walk, and not faint" (Isaiah 40:31, KJV). Patience, waiting, hope, faith—they weave that unique pattern of a person living under the lordship of Christ.

Of course, often there is no real choice but to wait; God sees to that. How we wait is all important. Some wait with fretting and worry, impatiently counting the hours or days, or anxiously anticipating an expected event. Some wait with stolid resignation, knowing God cannot be hurried, expecting the worst, hoping for the best. They live with a fatalistic view of life, devoid of joy and expectation. Some wait with a deep conviction of faith and a sure sense of God's good plan, joyfully certain that the outcome will bring glory to God.

How do you wait? In waiting you reveal the extent of Christ's lordship in your life. He is Lord of every event, and the timing of every event.

Not all waiting is for an event or a point in time. Some waiting, often the most difficult, is endurance in the midst of hard circumstances. "For you have need of endurance [patience], so that when you have done the will of God, you may receive what was promised" (Hebrews 10:36).

Endurance during trials and difficulties expresses faith and patience in a far deeper way than mere waiting for an expected event. Endurance produces character.

Consider it all joy, my brethren, when you encounter various trials, knowing that the testing of your faith produces endurance. And let endurance have its perfect result, that you may be perfect [mature] and complete, lacking in nothing. (James 1:2-4)

In Christ's lordship we wait for trials to end with no assurance that they will. So we endure with joy and confidence that He will supply the strength to endure. "Let us run with endurance the race that is set before us, fixing our eyes on

Jesus" (Hebrews 12:1-2). We wait and endure, knowing our times are in His hands (Psalm 31:5).

> There is an appointed time for everything.
> And there is a time for every event under heaven—
>> a time to give birth, and a time to die;
>> a time to plant, and a time to uproot what is planted;
>> a time to kill, and a time to heal;
>> a time to tear down, and a time to build up;
>> a time to weep, and a time to laugh;
>> a time to mourn, and a time to dance.
> (Ecclesiastes 3:1-4)

At all times Christ is Lord.

BEWARE, AND BE ON YOUR GUARD AGAINST
EVERY FORM OF GREED; FOR NOT EVEN
WHEN ONE HAS AN ABUNDANCE DOES HIS
LIFE CONSIST OF HIS POSSESSIONS.
Luke 12:15

16
Greed and Possessions: Deceptive Security

My mind grasps Jesus' warning against greed, but my emotions and my actions struggle with it daily. Since the first command— "You must not eat from the tree of the knowledge of good and evil"—greed has been a battleground of spiritual life. In each of us is an Achan lusting after the booty of Ai, a Solomon gathering riches, and even a Judas taking a bribe. We hate them all, yet tolerate their presence in our lives.

So many good things are spoiled by greed. A fine line divides legitimate desires from sinful greed. That line becomes clear only when the lordship of Christ comes to bear on those desires. The first line of battle against greed for most Christians relates to possessions and money. In life we focus first on security, then on accumulation and comfort. How many nights have I lain in bed and mentally calculated our family income and expenses? How many times have I received a small windfall of money and immediately began to dream of where to spend it on items I really didn't need? I recall my early fascination with stereo systems and other electronic gadgets that dented our family finances and blunted our giving. We each have our private areas of greed that regularly surface when a little extra money becomes available. One person's greed is another's privilege. In one area we can be relaxed and content, while in another we covet and lust.

I remember a faculty member at the Air Force Academy who daily was consumed with the rise or fall of the stock market. Others speculated in real estate. Still others focused their energies on career advancement. But almost all were motivated by a form of greed. The sequence goes something like this: security—greed—power—security. Security for the present. Greed for more of everything. Power for the ego. Security for the future.

The first basic drive after the survival instinct centers on material security in the present. We want money for food, a secure job, a house, and assurance of the basic necessities of life. This is normal and acceptable.

This security then spurs a greed for more: more money, more and better furniture, more house, more leisure, more vacations, more discretionary income, more prestige, more comfort, more security. This greed produces a lusting after money and the things it can buy. The lust then eats at one's basic value system, corrupting motives and actions. Ends justify means. The means and methods crowd out the deeper spiritual issues. Self-gratification then rules our lives.

Soon even material greed wears thin. How many rooms does one need? How many cars can one drive? How many clothes can one wear? Then another force begins to enter—power. After initial financial success and material security, the ego pursues power: power over people, power to control, power to change events. Such power intoxicates. It drives people to actions that they previously would have avoided. This power is not restricted to the wealthy or the executive. In every economic level men and women fight to gain a position of power: foreman over workers, church-committee chairman over members, parent over children, friend over friend.

Finally, there grows an acute awareness of age and mortality. Then a concern for security returns. How will I retire? How much money will I have? The brief encounter with power soon fades to a fear of the future and a panicky focus on retirement.

You may say that this is a perfect picture of the non-Christian, but I often see exactly the same pattern in Christians when the lordship of Christ is not a reality. Please do not misunderstand. Investing in the stock market is not wrong. Real estate speculation is not wrong. God gives the ability to make money, just as He gives an artist the ability to draw. Likewise, a basic desire for security is not wrong. What makes these things wrong is the *motive* for doing or seeking them. Usually that motive is greed and self-centeredness.

I see people who profess Christ exhibit an unhealthy striving for security, possessions, and power that ultimately leads them to lose spiritual hunger and discernment. They may even be faithful in many Christian basics and activities, yet be driven by motives of greed. How many Christians are captured by pyramid schemes of sales, promotions that ignore the emotional cost to the family, prosperity teaching that demands material and financial blessing from God? Others walk with God for years and then desperately seek security in their retirement years, out of greed, or at least because of fear.

We are all vulnerable. I can never expect that today's devotion to Christ's lordship will prevent tomorrow's submission to greed. With the disciples we pray, "And do not lead us into temptation, but deliver us from evil" (Matthew 6:13). The truth of 1 Timothy 6:9 must burn itself into our minds, "But those who *want* to get rich fall into temptation and a snare and many foolish and harmful desires which plunge men into ruin and destruction." Such greed causes ruin and destruction and can even lead people to wander away from the faith.

How many broken marriages have resulted from a sinful focus on greed for money and things? The husband's focus on money, job, or power, and the wife's focus on possessions and security—both sow the seeds of death in their marriage.

Christ wants to be Lord of our lives in this sensitive area of greed. Confess the need. Ask Him to be Lord and submit to His lordship. Without it, security is only a fleeting dream, giving way to a nightmare of life without His lordship. Let Christ be Lord.

> How blest is life if lived for Thee,
>   My loving Saviour and my Lord:
> No pleasures that the world can give
>   Such perfect gladness can afford.
>   —Author Unknown

LORD
OF MY
RELATIONSHIPS

17
Servanthood:
The Ultimate Expression
of Lordship

Most of us want to be prominent in something—to be recognized. That inner pride drives us all.

No one wants to be a servant. Servants are unobserved. They exist for another's comfort and convenience. They receive no recognition. Ancient kings had secret passageways and doors for the servants to move so they would not be seen.

Even in the Christian community, where servanthood is extolled, no one actually wants to be *treated* like a servant. The idea sounds great; the reality is miserable.

I have many opportunities to watch people in serving professions, as well as those who are served. Waiters, waitresses, porters, store clerks, flight attendants, janitors, and many others. I am angered by the treatment some give these servants—harsh words, snide comments, demanding attitudes, and abusive language. And the workers take it in silence. That's their job. They swallow their pride and take the abuse. I admire how so many of them keep their anger under control. Being a servant is not easy.

One of the ultimate tests of the lordship of Christ is our "servant quotient." If Jesus is our Lord, then, by definition, we are His servants—in fact, slaves. We were purchased by His blood—redeemed. Unlike slaves in human society, we can choose. But the choice is a "catch-22" choice. When we choose to be the bondservant of Jesus Christ, we enter into incomparable freedom. When we choose *not* to be His servant, we automatically choose to be a slave to the flesh and the world.

Most often that choice is not recognized, along with its tragic cost, until the best of life is spent. Then we regret the choice—to no avail—and we say, "If only I knew. . . ." But we do know. The Scriptures speak clearly:

> You know that the rulers of the Gentiles lord it over them, and their great men exercise authority over them. It is not so among you, but whoever wishes to become great among you shall be your servant, and whoever wishes to be first among you shall be your slave; just as the Son of Man did not come to be served, but to serve, and to give His life a ransom for many. (Matthew 20:25-28)

In God's eyes, greatness is servanthood.

Now we encounter some deceptive psychology. Who wouldn't want to be the servant of the president, or the queen, or some other head of state. Such people possess high status. So, being God's servant is not so loathsome. The catch? God's servant is automatically the servant to common, ordinary, sinful people. These people take advantage of servants, despise them, and never express appreciation.

True servants do not look for thanks or reward. Jesus taught that slaves who obey should expect no thanks but say, "We are unworthy slaves; we have done only that which we ought to have done" (Luke 17:10).

The lordship of Christ expresses itself in servanthood in two primary ways—*attitude* and *action*. Actions are relatively easy to see. Servants help other people. They see needs and meet them. They lift loads. They meet financial needs. They babysit, run errands, help in the home, take sick people to doctors, help others with their work. They serve those who can never repay and may never know the source of help.

Some have the gift of helping, and these actions come more naturally. For most Christians, serving requires a conscious effort. A servant does not spend all of his time looking for menial things to do for others, neglecting his regular work. Rather, he meets needs as he sees them in the normal course of life. He never thinks of any work as too menial or beneath his dignity or station in life. Servants can also lead, take responsibility, organize, or plan. They focus on the needs of others.

In The Navigators, servanthood has long been a major focus of training in discipleship. We try to teach men and women to look out first for the needs of others. The first steps of servanthood are often clumsy or obvious—opening doors, carrying luggage at a conference, working on a cleanup crew, or clearing the dinner table. In training environments servanthood seems natural. But in real life—on the job, in the home, at school, in the church—it becomes clear whether serving is a natural response or a forced activity.

Although actions are important, the heart of servanthood is in one's *attitude*. Do I possess the attitude of a servant? Do I serve from my heart or because I must? True servants hardly know they are serving. Service becomes an integral part of their lives.

Have you ever had someone serve you grudgingly—making you feel as if every act was a great imposition on his life? Or have you had someone serve in a mocking, insincere way—"Why, of course, Mr. White. Anything you say!" Such an attitude rings as true as a cracked bell. That is why Paul says, "Have this attitude in yourselves which was also in Christ Jesus" (Philippians 2:5).

We must join attitude and actions. One can serve and yet act like a haughty lord. One can be in a prominent position of power and authority and act like a true servant. This servant attitude only comes when one's life is truly yielded to the lordship of Christ.

Jesus Christ, the King of kings, became the Servant to servants. Can we become less?

Watch people in their unguarded moments. Are their responses that of a servant or of a superior? What are your responses?

The hardest test for me comes in my home. Will I truly serve my wife and children? Or do I resent their impositions on my private time? I confess to an internal battle there. I find it much easier to serve in my job, my ministry, and in my church. I still need to allow Christ's lordship to rule more in this area of my life.

But there is another side to the coin. Some people refuse to be served. They resist any attempts of others to meet their needs. Why? I believe the problem boils down to pride and independence. Peter refused to allow Christ to wash his feet. His pride and ego got in the way. Some refuse to be served in order to avoid an obligation to return the service. They keep a score book of deeds. Some people keep a social scorecard: "Lets see, the Johnsons asked us over, so now we need to have them over to our house" or "Alice gave a gift to our daughter when she graduated, so we had better do the same for their son." These attitudes spoil the grace of giving and serving. Not only do we need to learn to serve, but we need to learn to receive service gratefully and graciously, without a sense of obligation.

Have you ever been accused of being a servant? Why not? Perhaps there was not enough evidence to convict you.

Remember, you are *someone's* servant. Whose?

FOR I, TOO, AM A MAN UNDER AUTHORITY,
WITH SOLDIERS UNDER ME; AND I SAY TO
THIS ONE, "GO!" AND HE GOES, AND
TO ANOTHER, "COME!" AND HE COMES, AND
TO MY SLAVE, "DO THIS!" AND HE DOES IT.
Matthew 8:9

18
Authority:
The Test of Servanthood

Authority frightens and comforts. It guards and oppresses. It is hated and yet desperately needed.

Authority is one of the most misunderstood of attributes. When we want to accomplish a transaction with the government, we look for one in authority. When we want to do evil, we avoid those in authority.

The centurion in Matthew 8 understood authority. So did Jesus.

When Jesus arrived in Capernaum, a Roman army captain came and pled with him to come to his home and heal his servant boy who was in bed paralyzed and racked with pain.

"Yes," Jesus said, "I will come and heal him."

Then the officer said, "Sir, I am not worthy to have you in my home; [and it isn't necessary for you to come]. If you will only stand here and say, 'Be healed,' my servant will get well! I know, because I am under the authority of my superior officers and I have authority over my soldiers, and I say to one, 'Go,' and he goes, and to another, 'Come,' and he comes, and to my slave boy, 'Do this or that,' and he does it. And I know you have authority to tell his sickness to go—and it will go!"

Jesus stood there amazed! Turning to the crowd he said, "I haven't seen faith like this in all the land of Israel! And I tell you this, that many Gentiles [like this Roman officer], shall come from all over the world and sit down in the Kingdom of Heaven with Abraham, Isaac, and Jacob. And many an Israelite—those for whom the Kingdom was prepared—shall be cast into outer darkness, into the place of weeping and torment." (Matthew 8:5-12, TLB)

The Roman officer was both under authority and in authority. He clearly understood that no one could be an authority unto himself. He saw Jesus as both under God's authority and in a position of authority over the illness of his servant. All he wanted was Jesus' word of authority. The officer placed himself totally under Christ's authority by faith— and his faith is spoken of to this day. It even amazed Jesus.

How does this relate to the lordship of Jesus Christ in our lives? Many of our struggles stem from our response to authority—the authority inherent in government, employment, family, and the Christian community. How we respond is a direct reflection of our surrender to the lordship of Christ. Only under His lordship can we fully understand authority— or exercise it rightfully.

Under authority, we realize that we must respond in a

godly manner, even when such authority is incompetent or unjust. "Let every person be in subjection to the governing authorities. For there is no authority except from God, and those which exist are established by God" (Romans 13:1). Under the authority of Christ, we also come under the authority of those He has appointed. Governmental authorities, like all human authorities, are limited, and cannot force us to reject our faith or sin against our conscience, but those are extreme cases. Our problems usually arise in the day-to-day living under authority. There we are to submit with joy.

In our work we also face the hand of authority, often by incompetent, authoritarian, or greedy people. Yesterday a young believer shared his frustration with working for greedy, uncaring employers. "They don't care for anything but money. They cheat. They say my belief is just so much _____!" His vocabulary was a bit ripe, but his feelings reflected those of other Christians in the world.

Paul expressed it well:

> Slaves, in all things obey those who are your masters on
> earth, not with external service, as those who merely
> please men, but with sincerity of heart, fearing the Lord.
> Whatever you do, do your work heartily, as for the Lord
> rather than for men. (Colossians 3:22-23)

Authority in the family requires more than a passing comment. Perhaps the charge to "be subject to one another in the fear of Christ" (Ephesians 5:21) says it best. We must recognize rightful authority of husbands and wives and parents. Only in that context will a family function in peace and love. Conflict never glorifies God.

A godly response to authority begins in the home. A child who learns obedience to parents will more easily adjust to authorities in other contexts. That pattern is set by how the husband and wife relate to each other. If they rebel at each other's authority, so will the children. The meaning and implications of submission and love in marriage need to be understood. The husband is responsible to love and lead. The wife also leads, but in response to her husband's authority. The dominance of either presents an unbalanced view of authority to the children, as well as leading to a misuse of authority in the marriage.

A much more sensitive area is authority in the church and the Christian community. The question is, authority over what? Certainly it is not authority over every area of our lives. I do not subscribe to the concept of authority which sets legalistic "dos and don'ts" for living.

Spiritual authority can reside in three entities—a person, a position, or a community of believers. In each case, no authority can be exercised without permission. That is different from the authority of government or family—although even there one must place himself under that authority voluntarily before redemptive authority (as opposed to disciplinary authority) can be experienced. Spiritual authority is expressed primarily through leadership. (See also 1 Corinthians 16:15-18.)

> Obey your leaders, and submit to them; for they keep
> watch over your souls, as those who will give an account.
> Let them do this with joy and not with grief, for this
> would be unprofitable for you. (Hebrews 13:17)

The primary functions of leadership in the church are to teach the Scriptures faithfully, to confront sin, to encourage personal growth to maturity and holy living, and to lead in the orderly responsibilities of the church—evangelism, caring for personal needs, and discipling.

We submit to the authority of a person as they demonstrate a godly walk and are willing to invest in another's life as a mentor. We submit to the authority of one in a position of responsibility as an elder or pastor-leader. Both of these are governed by Hebrews 13:7, "Remember those who led you, who spoke the word of God to you; and considering the result of their conduct, imitate their faith." One should never submit blindly.

Finally, there is authority in the community of believers as we agree to be a part of a team of believers in a local body. In that context we permit others to guide us with authority in a limited range of our lives.

All of these authorities can be, and likely will be, misused. Yet they are legitimate. In Christ's lordship we submit as He leads us. He will use each of these authorities to guide and develop us.

On the other hand, we may be one of those *in authority* over others, either Christians or nonChristians. In exercising our authority we bear a great responsibility to demonstrate Christ's lordship.

In government we must be just and honest with all, remembering that we are servants of the people.

In the world of work, we must exercise fairness and kindness: "Masters, grant to your slaves justice and fairness, knowing that you too have a Master in heaven" (Colossians 4:1). We should treat others as we would wish to be treated by our superiors. Do those who work under you see that clear expression of the lordship of Christ in your life and actions?

In the family, we exercise authority that strongly affects another's inner being and personhood. How deeply we can hurt our children or spouse by the unthinking exercise of legitimate authority! Husbands and parents bear a responsibility of a spiritual authority unlike any other since it is *always* exercised—rightly or wrongly. Our surrender to the lordship of Christ will give us the wisdom and sensitivity to lead spiritually in our family.

Spiritual leadership and authority demands depth in our

lordship commitment beyond all other areas of authority. We have no *right* to lead; we do so out of love and obedience. We lead not for adulation, but for the good of others. We must lead and exercise authority with the care of a skilled surgeon. We must never act out of selfishness or pride. If we do not meet the requirements for a particular leadership role, we cannot allow ourselves to be thrust into it—especially when the lack is of a spiritual nature. We must examine ourselves. As we lead, we need to take great care not to overstep the boundaries of our authority—especially the authority that another has granted to us over his life. Humility in authority should permeate our actions and influence.

Whether *under* or *in* authority, we can meet the difficult demands only when our total motive is to live under the authority of our Lord Jesus Christ. Only in His lordship can our motives and responses reflect holiness and godliness in the exercise of authority.

IF ANYONE DOES NOT STUMBLE IN WHAT HE SAYS,
HE IS A PERFECT MAN, ABLE TO BRIDLE THE
WHOLE BODY AS WELL. . . . BUT NO ONE CAN TAME
THE TONGUE; IT IS A RESTLESS EVIL
AND FULL OF DEADLY POISON.
James 3:2, 8

19
The Tongue:
Betrayer of the Heart

Do you remember the old school children's taunt, "Sticks and stones may break my bones, but words can never hurt me"? Nothing is farther from the truth. Words cut. They maim and kill in a way that lasts for a lifetime. Words hurled in anger live on in the mind. Whether hurled at us or by us, they haunt our minds and our dreams. They can never be retrieved. What was said remains forever in the eternity of the mind.

Though we have all been hurt deeply by unkind words and though we know the pain they cause, yet we still lash out at others, as if in retaliation. Our best efforts at restraint often fade in the emotion of the moment. The truth of James 3:8 is demonstrated daily in our lives: the tongue is, indeed, a restless evil and full of deadly poison.

Children are brutally honest. "That's an ugly dress," a child will say. Teens are often cynical. "Do you like that dress better than what is in fashion today?" a teenage girl might ask. Adults become subtle. "Have you ever had your coloring analyzed for wardrobe coordination?" Each type of comment gets the message across.

How I wish I could take back words I have said in anger or haste—to my children, my wife, my coworkers! Apologies help, but they apply only a necessary salve on a wound hastily made.

"Like apples of gold in settings of silver is a word spoken in right circumstances" (Proverbs 25:11). With the tongue we can praise God and encourage a friend. We can comfort and give wise suggestions. We can teach God's Word and point people to obedience. We can share the truth of the gospel and persuade men and women to believe.

How can we bring the lordship of Christ to bear on this unruly member of our body?

Perhaps more than any other external evidence, the tongue reveals the depth of the lordship of Christ in the heart. Jesus taught, "For the mouth speaks out of that which fills the heart" (Matthew 12:34). The battle of the tongue rages first in the heart. What resides in the heart pours out through the mouth.

And the mind is the door to the heart. What flows into the mind fills the heart. Evil thoughts, lustful fantasies, jealousy, and envy comprise only a small list of sins that invade our minds, corrupt our hearts, and find their expression in words. Anger in words would never appear if it were not first in thoughts in our hearts. Cutting remarks find their roots in thoughts of envy and jealousy that seek either revenge or hurt to another. Thus the solution lies in nurturing a heart of love and concern for others.

"The good man out of the good treasure of his heart brings forth what is good . . . for his mouth speaks from that which fills his heart" (Luke 6:45). How does one fill the heart with that which is good? The first obvious step is the realization that no one is "good" until they are first made righteous through personal salvation in Christ. The root must first be holy, possible only in Christ. Then comes the care and feeding of a "good heart." The basic ingredient is God's Word, the Scriptures energized by the Holy Spirit. We must daily feed on the Word to nurture the heart. How is your daily intake of Scripture? Do you spend time with God regularly in reading, meditation, and prayer? Without such a practice the battle of the heart and tongue can never be won.

But like growing food in a garden, there will be no fruit without work. The desire for fruit must be accompanied by the discipline of cultivation. Ultimately, the tongue is controlled by discipline—both over what enters the heart and what the tongue says.

Proverbs aptly instructs, "Watch over your heart with all diligence, for from it flow the springs of life" (Proverbs 4:23). Casual desire will not do, only deliberate, constant diligence. What you read, what you think and what you see all feed the heart. All require decisions of the will. This passage continues:

> Put away from you a deceitful mouth, and put devious lips far from you. Let your eyes look directly ahead, and let your gaze be fixed straight in front of you. Watch the path of your feet. (Proverbs 4:24-26)

All of these warnings require discipline. No one can do it for you.

The psalmist prayed, "Set a guard, O LORD, over my mouth; keep watch over the door of my lips" (Psalm 141:3). He knew the danger of an undisciplined tongue and the need for help from God to control it. "Guard" and "watch"—words of discipline. Discipline ensures the feeding of the mind and heart with the right food. Then the discipline of the tongue becomes possible.

Is discipline of the tongue only a stoic silencing of an unruly instrument? Do we live our lives in monastic silence to keep from the sin of words? Hardly! The tongue is a great healer—an instrument of love and comfort. Paul urged, "Let no unwholesome word proceed from your mouth, but only such a word as is good for edification according to the need of the moment, that it may give grace to those who hear" (Ephesians 4:29). We want our tongues to bless and encourage, to comfort and uplift, to soothe and edify.

"Death and life are in the power of the tongue," says Proverbs 18:21. Under the lordship of Christ, our lips will minister life.

BUT I SAY TO YOU WHO HEAR,
LOVE YOUR ENEMIES,
DO GOOD TO THOSE WHO HATE YOU,
BLESS THOSE WHO CURSE YOU,
PRAY FOR THOSE WHO MISTREAT YOU.
Luke 6:27-28

20
Enemies:
Overcoming Prejudice

Near the end of World War II Okinawa was under siege. Swarms of young Marines swept onto the beach under heavy fire. In their midst was a tall Marine, Bob Boardman. Suddenly Japanese bullets hit him, piercing his throat and clipping off part of a finger. The bullet permanently damaged his vocal cords, reducing his speech to a whisper for the rest of his life.

Bob was one of thousands who survived maimed, but alive. Many soldiers developed a deep, lifelong hatred for the enemy, but not Bob. He was a new Christian. After the war came hospitals and rehabilitation and a deep involvement with The Navigators. He became impressed with the need of the world for the gospel. He developed a heart for the Japanese people; he began to love his enemies.

Mission boards discouraged him, saying that with his hoarse whisper he would never be able to speak the language. But he persisted. After more than 30 years in Japan, Bob left a healthy, growing ministry in Japanese hands. He gave his life for his former enemies.

Could you do that? Could you give your life to those who hated you and mistreated you? This is Jesus' direct command: "Love your enemies" (Luke 6:27). It's hard enough to love your friends or even those whom you do not know. But to love an enemy, that is almost impossible. This is one of the greatest tests of lordship, because it is so contrary to human nature. To tolerate? Possibly. To love? Impossible—apart from the power of the indwelling Christ.

There are two categories of enemies—group and personal. We all grow up with a set of prejudices; we develop others through bitter experience. Race, social class, profession, wealth, and personality are breeding grounds for classes of enemies. Whites, blacks, Jews, Arabs, Communists make up only a partial list of enemy classes. Try as we may, we tend to view those of other groups as enemies for whom love is difficult—if not impossible.

Jesus set the pace when He broke tradition to reach out to the Samaritan woman. In one of His parables Jesus also made a Samaritan, the archenemy of the Jews, a hero, the example of love for one's neighbor.

Race and nationality barriers are relatively easy to see and deal with. But other group hatreds are not so easy. Consider the enmity between physicians and chiropractors, conservatives and liberals, rich and poor, uneducated and educated, managers and workers, Catholic and Protestant. No one is immune to feelings of prejudice and hatred. You may say, "They are not really enemies, just competitors." Whatever the degree of dislike or distance, they do not fall into the category of those we love. But under the lordship of Christ, we are to love them, whether they are Christian or nonChristian. They are people who need Christ and who need God's love.

How do we respond to people who come from a group that is opposed to our profession or ideals? We need to examine our inner heart's response to the "Samaritans" in our lives.

The even more difficult enemies to love are the ones we know personally. Hatred and dislike erupt in our relationships. People wrong us and try to hurt us. In some cases the hurt is so deep and personal that it almost precludes any thoughts of love. A boss who unjustly fires us, an estranged spouse, a business competitor who has dealt unethically, a neighbor with whom conflict has existed for years, a business partner who becomes antagonistic, a friend who spreads hurtful gossip, someone you wronged who will not forgive you—all of these people can become objects of hatred. Relationships with people like this tear us up emotionally and poison us for years as the gall of bitterness infects us.

Often we try to avoid these people and forget them altogether. But the memory returns, and sometimes we then seek subtle ways of personal revenge.

What should we do? The Scriptures speak clearly on the issue, but its instruction is not easy to apply.

First, admit that the enmity for the person or group exists and that it is wrong. This may be the hardest step. Jesus' primary teaching comes from Luke 6:27-28: "But I say to you who hear, love your enemies, do good to those who hate you, bless those who curse you, pray for those who mistreat you." Love can come only from God. But you can pray for the good of an enemy, not their hurt. It is hard to pray for someone and hate them at the same time. Pray for their salvation. If they are Christians, pray for their walk with God and for conviction regarding sin.

King David did not learn this lesson. He was a man after God's own heart, but as he grew older, he became vindictive, seeking revenge. In the psalms David condemns his enemies and asks for vengeance against them. He did not love his enemies.

Jesus introduced that love in His teaching. He set a new pattern for the future. In this context Jesus gave the famed Golden Rule: "Just as you want men to treat you, treat them in the same way" (Luke 6:31).

Put yourself in an enemy's place. How would you want to be treated? Jesus continues:

> And if you love those who love you, what credit is that to you? For even sinners love those who love them. And if you do good to those who do good to you, what credit is that to you? For even sinners do the same.
> (Luke 6:32-33)

The Christian lives by a higher standard. So Jesus repeats, "But love your enemies, and do good, and lend, expecting nothing in return; and your reward will be great" (6:35). Can we believe this promise? Will God actually reward us? That is what He says. Jesus does not specify what He will do. He may not solve the problem immediately, but He will work.

Jesus gives the most compelling reason for this attitude, "For He Himself is kind to ungrateful and evil men. Be merciful, just as your Father is merciful" (6:35-36). The pattern is God Himself: He loved us even when we rebelled against Him.

Paul teaches similarly in Romans 12:17-20:

> Never pay back evil for evil to anyone. Respect what is right in the sight of all men. If possible, so far as it depends on you, be at peace with all men. Never take your own revenge, beloved, but leave room for the wrath of God, for it is written, "Vengeance is mine, I will repay," says the Lord. "But if your enemy is hungry, feed him, and if he is thirsty, give him a drink; for in so doing you will heap burning coals upon his head."

We are never permitted revenge. As we obey God, He will convict the person of sin (the "burning coals"). Our motive is not to heap burning coals on them, but to demonstrate the love of God.

Consider another issue. What if we are at fault? What if we caused the enmity? After all, there are always two sides to every conflict, and rarely is one side without any fault. You may need to ask forgiveness and make things right with someone—and with God.

Your response may be, "Well, so much for that theory." But don't write God off in this matter. You believe Him in other areas, why not here? Yes, it is hard. Pride must be swallowed. But in the end, peace will result.

Merle Meeter reflects on "Dissension":

> How it lances the chest,
> Rasps the walls of the stomach:
> hacking,
> corrosive,
> Rash and livid to slash,
> Shrill and straining to crush.
>
> Trust in the Lord and His Word
> Flung away—wrathful ego rampant,
> murderous,
> suicidal—
> The face of the King on the coin
> Of the heart gouged and gashed.[1]

May God give us the courage to love even our enemies.

NOTE:
1. Merle Meeter, "Dissension," *The Country of the Risen King* (Grand Rapids: Baker Book House, 1978), page 133.

AND A LEPER CAME TO HIM, BESEECHING HIM
AND FALLING ON HIS KNEES BEFORE HIM.
Mark 1:40

21
Loving People I Don't Like

A leper and a demon-possessed maniac—two people no one would choose to associate with, especially in Jesus' day. Both were outcasts of society. Jesus allowed both to come to Him. Likely they grabbed His garments or legs as they kneeled (Mark 1:40-44, 5:1-20).

Consider Peter or Judas. Neither of these men were particularly lovable. Peter blustered about like a bull in a china shop. Judas sneaked about, stealing from the common pot, and ultimately betrayed Jesus.

The leper came and pleaded for healing. Jesus "stretched out His hand, and touched him, and said to him, 'I am willing; be cleansed'" (Mark 1:41). In an instant, before their eyes, the leprosy disappeared, and the man was clean.

In Mark 5 the demon-possessed man from the Gerasene country ran out of the tombs. At night people heard his eerie wailing as he threw himself about and gashed himself with stones. The man could not even speak. Rather the demons spoke, "What do I have to do with You, Jesus, Son of the Most High God?" (Mark 5:7).

Think of the scene. The maniac is grasping Christ's robe. His eyes are frantic, his hair matted with blood and dirt. His clothes, such as they were, smelled of the tombs and sweat and blood.

Jesus welcomed him and healed him. The people came "and observed the man who had been demon-possessed sitting down, clothed and in his right mind" (Mark 5:15).

How did Jesus do it? How could He endure so many difficult people? How can we? Or should we?

A part of living under the lordship of Christ is allowing unlovable people into our lives, people whom we would never choose on our own. They enter our lives, often like a storm, disturbing our tranquility and testing our patience.

Paul gives us some guidelines on dealing with these people:

Now we who are strong ought to bear the weaknesses of those without strength and not just please ourselves. Let each of us please his neighbor for his good, to his edification. . . . Wherefore, accept one another, just as Christ also accepted us to the glory of God. (Romans 15:1-2,7)

The first requisite for loving the unlovable is to realize how Christ accepted you. Where would you be today without Him? What if His acceptance had been conditional? Realize that right now Christ fully accepts you as you are, full of imperfections and problems, all of which He knows completely.

The second emerges from a basic decision to accept

everyone God brings across your path. In God's plan there are no accidental meetings. In each encounter God has a purpose for both the needy person and for you. You may be the one who can really help and counsel that person.

Determine to be an encouragement to everyone whom God brings across your path. It costs little to say a kind word and to communicate a sense of support. But like the girl who doesn't want to encourage a suitor, we fear that kind words will lead to further demands. Such is the risk.

One great help to me is to recall how people hurt me. As a young high school student, I remember a particularly painful interview with a Navy captain. I traveled by train from Spokane, Washington, to Seattle. There I stayed at the YMCA. I knew no one in the city. At stake was a Navy ROTC scholarship that would pay part of my university education. I was nervous and self-conscious. My white shirt was one of those old drip-dry kind with the collar wrinkled and looking just like what it was—a cheap shirt. My blue suit was, at best, acceptable. My black shoes were old-fashioned. It was clear that I did not come from a socially conscious home. I knew just enough to know that I didn't look quite right.

The interview is still painful to recall. I felt very put down. In my application I had stated that I liked music. The Navy captain began to ask questions about classical music. Where was Bach born? I didn't know. And so it went through the interview. It was disastrous. He put a negative recommendation on my record, and I was not selected.

The captain may not have intended to intimidate me. He probably was doing his job—picking the most poised and the one with the best leadership potential. I think I was at least in the "unlikable" class. That memory helps me remember not to put anyone down because of how they look or their lack of poise.

Through the years others have so graciously put up with

my pestering personality. I asked skeptical questions in college classes. I'm certain I exasperated my professors. In my early years with The Navigators, I know I was abrasive and demanding. Many of my friends graciously ignored these signs, helping me to grow. I am grateful for those who were patient with me. Even today, I know that I can irritate people of a particular personality type, yet they accept me.

I appreciate the instruction of Hebrews 13.

> Keep on loving each other as brothers. Do not forget to entertain strangers, for by so doing some people have entertained angels without knowing it. Remember those in prison as if you were their fellow prisoners, and those who are mistreated as if you yourselves were suffering. (Hebrews 13:1-3, NIV)

We never know where a kindness will lead, because only God can see the potential of that man or woman in our presence.

Through the years, my wife and I have encountered many people in our ministry who were not easy to love. Yet today we see many who are in places of responsibility both in the secular and Christian world. They grew and developed. God worked in their lives and burnished the rough edges. What a blessing to see them today!

May God help me to totally love and accept every person He brings across my path, as Christ totally loves and accepts me. May He bring my human responses under His lordship.

LORD OF MY GIFTS AND ABILITIES

FOR THROUGH THE GRACE GIVEN TO ME I SAY
TO EVERY MAN AMONG YOU NOT TO THINK
MORE HIGHLY OF HIMSELF THAN HE
OUGHT TO THINK; BUT TO THINK SO AS
TO HAVE SOUND JUDGMENT, AS GOD HAS
ALLOTTED TO EACH A MEASURE OF FAITH.
AND SINCE WE HAVE GIFTS THAT DIFFER
ACCORDING TO THE GRACE GIVEN TO US,
LET EACH EXERCISE THEM ACCORDINGLY.
Romans 12:3,6

22
Gifts and Abilities:
A Question of Ownership

When I speak publicly, I realize that no matter how well-prepared I am, the effectiveness of the message rests with God. As I begin speaking, I see the audience begin to respond. A touching illustration gets attention. Then I begin to sense that my words cut into peoples' hearts with power, and I begin to be proud. I think that *I* have put together a great message. Suddenly ego has replaced dependence on God.

A soloist stands in front of a congregation. He begins to sing—or to perform. The line between performing and serving can easily blur as public recognition increases.

Athletic ability, teaching gifts, leadership skills, personality, appearance, or intellectual capacity—all can be used by God, but all can engender pride. Even the gift of helping can be misused to draw attention to itself.

The people of Corinth were the most gifted of all the New Testament churches, but they became proud and immoral. Clearly, their gifts and abilities were not surrendered to the lordship of Jesus Christ. Those most gifted and talented cannot contribute to the Kingdom of God without total surrender to His lordship.

In a practical way how does one surrender gifts and abilities to the lordship of Christ? Certainly a brief prayer of surrender cannot turn the ego and pride of self into a consistently surrendered humility. Rather, we pursue a path of surrender, a series of deliberate decisions that gradually crucify the inner selfish motives of the gifted and talented.

Begin with the honest admission that no gift or talent springs from any good or merit in yourself. The very use of the word "gift" implies a valued asset deposited in your life by another. Clearly affirm that feelings of superiority rest on no foundation in reality. You had nothing to do with your birth, genetic heritage, social circumstances, intelligence, or spiritual gifts. God gave them to you. Nothing short of total admission of your debt and dependence will do. You neither earned nor deserve any abilities that seem to be such a central expression of your being. Consequently, pride and ego are ludicrous at best. Yet they reside in the heart, hammering out the lie, "I am the sole source of all my gifts and talents." No one wishes to admit dependence, especially for that part of self that so clearly becomes synonymous with one's identity.

Your only choice rests in what you do with what you have been given. Every spiritual gift and every ability focuses on one purpose—to serve: "But to each one is given the manifestation of the Spirit for the *common good*" (1 Corinthians 12:7). The benefit of one's gifts must accrue to the Body of Christ, and, beyond that, to all the human race. Peter communicated a similar thought: "As each one has received a special gift, employ it in serving one another, as good stewards of the manifold grace of God" (1 Peter 4:10). "Employ as good stewards" implies a responsibility for something that does not belong to the steward. A gift is to be used primarily for service.

Why then do Christians take glory in their gifts? Why do they act as though they created them within themselves? They are motivated to serve themselves rather than to serve God and others. Surrender requires servanthood, using our God-created gifts and abilities for the benefit of others.

When true surrender of gifts and abilities to the lordship of Christ occurs, there will be a *willingness not to misuse* that gift or ability. Each of us possesses gifts that may not be expressed at all times. Some gifts require maturity, which emerges with years of walking with God. Other gifts need submerging in our lives until certain areas of need are met. Deeper issues of character take priority over the immediate expression of gifts.

I find that some of my abilities are often not used for periods of months or even years. Family demands, job pressures, and other spiritual responsibilities preempt the time and opportunity to use aspects of my abilities. As life becomes more focused, we find that we may need to surrender some areas of ability that we really enjoy expressing.

Similarly, surrender can mean a willingness to perform tasks that lie outside your gifts. Sometimes we refuse to attempt tasks not directly related to our gifts and abilities, yet serving in the Body of Christ demands a commitment to serve the need, not use gifts. Whether or not we possess the gift of helping, floors need scrubbing, dishes need washing, and people need feeding. We can fill the need. We should not abandon our gifts to meet random "needs," but we can willingly serve people in whatever manner the Holy Spirit indicates.

The subtle pull of pride expresses itself in the desire for recognition. Can we serve and express God-given gifts when we receive no recognition? True servanthood requires no recognition except from God alone. God graciously allows recognition and acclaim to come, but we cannot demand it, nor expect it. The glory must go to God, not us. When we receive no recognition and begin to resent it, we catch a glimpse of our deepest motivations. We must surrender our need and desire for recognition.

Surrender—so difficult when it touches the point of ego. Only one motivation can overpower our human reluctance: the glory of God. Every expression of our gifts and abilities must point to God Himself. He says, "I am the LORD, that is My name; I will not give My glory to another, nor My praise to graven images" (Isaiah 42:8). God speaks directly to the matter of abilities in Jeremiah 9:23-24:

> Let not a wise man boast of his wisdom, and let not
> the mighty man boast of his might, let not a rich man
> boast of his riches; but let him who boasts boast of this,
> that he understands and knows Me, that I am the LORD
> who exercises lovingkindness, justice, and righteousness
> on earth; for I delight in these things.

How do we give glory to God? We can say, "I want to give God the glory." However, the most powerful statement emerges not from words, but from life. The way we live, our devotion to God, and our attitude bear witness to God's glory more than any words. Just as Moses' face shone, without his knowing it, so our lives will unknowingly reflect that deep inner walk cultivated in hours and days spent living under the lordship of Christ.

We can pray the words of the following poem:

> I do not ask
> That crowds may throng the temple,

That standing room be at a price;
I only ask that as I voice the message
They may see Christ.

I do not ask
For churchly pomp or pageant,
Or music such as wealth alone can buy;
I only ask that as I voice the message,
He may be nigh.

I do not ask
For earthly place or council,
Or of this world's distinction any part;
I only ask when I have voiced the message,
My Saviour's heart.

I do not ask
That men may sound my praises,
Or headlines spread my name abroad;
I only pray that as I voice the message,
Hearts may find God.

       —Author Unknown

THE KING REFLECTED AND SAID, "IS THIS
NOT BABYLON THE GREAT, WHICH I MYSELF
HAVE BUILT AS A ROYAL RESIDENCE BY
THE MIGHT OF MY POWER AND FOR THE
GLORY OF MY MAJESTY?"
Daniel 4:30

23
Success:
Lordship in the Limelight

Nebuchadnezzar had it made—power, success, achievement, position, and a godly advisor, Daniel. Nebuchadnezzar created one of the seven wonders of the ancient world, the Hanging Gardens of Babylon. He built streets more than forty feet wide. He reigned as king for forty-three years. He ruled with fear and terror.

He was also a dreamer who demanded to know the meaning of his dreams. Once he demanded not only the interpretation of the dream from the astrologers and so-called wise men, but also the content of the dream itself. Their success ended. Nebuchadnezzar suspected their fakery and ordered them all executed.

Daniel saved the day by doing the impossible: he related

the dream and its interpretation. Before Daniel gave the interpretation, he told the king the true source of his wisdom:

> Let the name of God be blessed forever and ever, for wisdom and power belong to Him. And it is He who changes the times and the epochs; He removes kings and establishes kings; He gives wisdom to wise men, and knowledge to men of understanding . . . To Thee, O God of my fathers, I give thanks and praise . . . for Thou hast made known to us the king's matter. (Daniel 2:20-23)

Thirty-two years later Nebuchadnezzar called on him to interpret another vision. This one was terrible, and Daniel was shaken. Daniel warned the king to repent: "Break away now from your sins by doing righteousness, and from your iniquities by showing mercy to the poor" (4:27).

The king ignored the warning. Twelve months later, on the roof of the royal palace, he boasted of how he had built Babylon by his own power and for his own glory (4:30). The story continues:

> Immediately the word concerning Nebuchadnezzar was fulfilled; and he was driven away from mankind and began eating grass like cattle, and his body was drenched with the dew of heaven, until his hair had grown like eagles' feathers and his nails like birds' claws. (Daniel 4:33)

His insanity lasted for seven years, until he repented and acknowledged God.

No one can take God's glory. But like Nebuchadnezzar, how easy it is to think our success results from our own doing. We need not focus on the nonbeliever and his boasting in pride; God will deal with him eventually. Rather, we should consider ourselves and other believers who experience success.

We need to cry out to God for help in success as well as in
failure or trouble. We need to surrender our success to the
lordship of Jesus Christ. We can lay no claim to credit for
our success. Paul asks some penetrating questions:

> What are you so puffed up about? What do you have that
> God hasn't given you? And if all you have is from God,
> why act as though you are so great, and as though you
> have accomplished something on your own?
> (1 Corinthians 4:7, TLB)

God remains the source of all our abilities and successes.
The best perspective on success comes either from times of
failure or from years of surrender to His lordship prior to
the success. Then the foundation of a deep walk with God will
undergird our lives and confront the temptations of success.

Whether your walk with God springs from new experience
or years of dependence, acknowledge Him and give Him glory
now. Do it daily. Do it publicly, not always in words, but by
a humility of spirit which only Christ can generate.

Both success and failure produce dangers. Failure can
lead to bitterness, and success can lead to pride. We have a
dilemma. When success comes, is it wrong to be pleased and
proud of an accomplishment, a promotion, or an award? No,
not all that we call pride is sinful. We certainly ought to say
to our children, "I am very proud of you," when they achieve
and succeed. We can be deeply pleased—even proud—that our
work bore fruit, our accomplishments publicly acknowledged.
The pattern of sinful pride invades when we begin thinking
"I did it" and believe that God contributed little.

Another sign of sinful pride appears when we look down
on others who do not experience success, accomplishment,
or promotion. Then we need to remember Paul's words: "Do
nothing from selfishness or empty conceit, but with humility

of mind let each of you regard one another as more important than himself" (Philippians 2:3).

We all want to succeed at what we do—work, family, or Christian service. No one wants to fail. But a striving for success can be exceedingly costly. When success consumes us, the focus of our life changes from God's glory to our own glory. The tragic truth is that most people strive for success in the wrong arenas and discover their error too late. The prideful push to succeed, even for good things, eats like a cancer in the spiritual life. It consumes the mind and occupies valuable time. It finally leaves us empty, whether we succeed or not. In its pursuit, the family suffers, health suffers, and spiritual growth is stunted.

However, success surrendered to the lordship of Christ can bring great glory to God: "Do you see a man skilled in his work? He will serve before kings; he will not serve before obscure men" (Proverbs 22:29, NIV). History abounds with stories of men and women whose success and achievements were used greatly by God for witness and for the social good of humankind. Parliamentarian William Wilberforce, scientist Isaac Newton, United Nation's Secretary General Dr. Charles Malik, and manufacturer R.G. LeTourneau exerted great influence for God and used their success for His glory. God takes some people of ability and promotes them to positions of great influence. Joseph became second only to the Pharaoh in Egypt in order to preserve the nation of Israel. Like Queen Esther, God placed him in a position "for such a time as this" (Esther 4:14).

When God gives success we can rejoice in it and enjoy it, knowing and acknowledging God as the source. We ought not to reject success or position any more than we should seek it. If we daily surrender ourselves to Christ's lordship, God will place us wherever He wishes in this world.

Only by His grace and power can we encounter success

and position and use it for His glory instead of our own pride and ego.

If success has been your goal and god to this point, surrender it to God now. Embark today on a new path of humble submission to Christ, changing whatever in your life springs from pride and ego. After you have begun to change your actions and motives, publicly acknowledge your decision.

BUT WE URGE YOU, BRETHREN, TO EXCEL
STILL MORE, AND TO MAKE IT YOUR
AMBITION TO LEAD A QUIET LIFE AND
ATTEND TO YOUR OWN BUSINESS AND WORK
WITH YOUR HANDS, JUST AS WE COMMANDED
YOU; SO THAT YOU MAY BEHAVE PROPERLY
TOWARD OUTSIDERS AND NOT BE IN ANY NEED.
1 Thessalonians 4:10-12

24
Work:
The Conflict of
Necessity and Desire

Why work? To make money to buy food to keep healthy, to work and make more money? Such a futile circle of life only makes the question more desperate.

Most people, Christians included, plod through life tolerating their work, wondering where it will lead and why it gives so little fulfillment. Work in the office, factory, or home so easily becomes a dull, draining necessity, with little or no eternal purpose. We work because we must.

To live an effective Christian life in the marketplace demands daily surrender to the lordship of Christ in several areas of life.

The most fundamental surrender is to admit that God wants you where you are now. Whether the job thrills you or bores you, recognize that God placed you there. Even if greed and ego persuaded you to take a job, or when you believe that God may be leading you into a vocational change, quietly agree to stay, and patiently allow God to work. Running and escaping can lead us out of the frying pan and into the fire.

We need the willingness to work hard. "Whatever you do, do your work heartily, as for the Lord rather than for men" (Colossians 3:23). Hard work is different from workaholism. Workaholics work feverishly for long hours to the neglect of other priorities and for improper reasons. Good workers work hard when they work, but they do not develop a dependence on the job for self-esteem.

A lazy Christian gives cause for the gospel of Christ to be maligned and discredited. All too many nonChristians decry the disparity between Christians' profession of religion and the reality of their work and family lives. A lazy Christian worker will never build a basis for sharing the gospel. There will be a testimony—there always is—but it will be a negative, destructive testimony.

Regrets from the past often creep in and spoil a person's satisfaction on the job. This is especially true for a new believer. Tom came to know Christ in mid-life. He had no education beyond high school. His job was frustrating and boring, but he was trapped. He began to reflect on his failure to get further education. Regret set in. He wanted to redo his past, but he could not. He had to come to grips with God's sovereignty over the past and face Christ's lordship in his current circumstances. Each of us can easily fall into the trap of regret which spoils the blessings of God in today's work.

Perhaps you have dealt with these issues already, but we all battle with one issue daily—our abilities. People are not created equal in ability and intellect. People have equal value, but not equal ability. The believer faces this issue at two extremes. One extreme finds the person unwilling to admit and use the abilities God gave. The other extreme is the un-willingness to admit certain limitations of ability. The first person looks down on himself, degrades his talents, and refuses to attempt certain tasks in his job. The latter person refuses to admit that he cannot do something. Failure in promotion or accomplishment always gets blamed on circumstances or other people, whereas the truth may lie in lack of ability.

Romans 12:3 teaches that a person ought "not to think more highly of himself than he ought to think; but to think so as to have sound judgment." The Phillips translation says we are to have "a sane estimate" of our capabilities: Under Christ's lordship we can, but independently, we always misjudge our-selves. We need to know our abilities and live within them.

When we truly possess certain abilities, but our employer or supervisor does not recognize them or refuses to use them, our commitment to Christ's lordship is tested. Our sense of failure and justice is aroused, and sometimes we can do nothing to change the situation.

This brings us to the issues of religious persecution and unfair treatment. Both can occur, but we must distinguish between them.

Persecution comes when bad treatment relates directly to our Christian testimony. Although persecution is a common occurrence in many countries today, it rarely happens in the free world. Often what is regarded as persecution simply results from a Christian's inability to relate in a nonChristian environment. Christians at work often witness in a foolish or unwise manner. Obvious symbols, pins, and plaques seldom help. Confrontive witnessing, in which no relationship or friendship exists, usually closes the door to future witness. What passes for witness may be little more than salving one's own con-science, allowing one to say, "I have witnessed." Such actions can bring professional repercussions, but it is not persecution.

Use 1 Peter 3:15-17 (NIV) as a guide:

But in your hearts set apart Christ as Lord. Always be prepared to give an answer to everyone who asks you to give the reason for the hope that you have. But do this with gentleness and respect, keeping a clear conscience, so that those who speak maliciously against your good behavior in Christ may be ashamed of their slander. It is better, if it is God's will, to suffer for doing good than for doing evil.

People should see your hope and then ask. Our reply should communicate Christ with gentleness and respect, not with argument and contention. Be known by your good *work* and your good *works*, not by religious idiosyncrasies.

Unfair treatment is not always the same as persecution. Some supervisors and employers simply treat people unfairly as a matter of course. So we suffer. We may be singled out for bad treatment for many other reasons than our Christian testimony. Under Christ's lordship, we should take such treatment in the spirit of 1 Peter 2:20 and patiently endure. God will reward and bless in His time and His way.

The Scriptures command the believer to do good, to do what is right, to be honest. But the world of business does not always follow those standards. Living under Christ's lordship at work means living in honesty under God's standard of ethics. Cheating, stealing, lying, and misrepresentation occur so commonly they hardly command notice. But after we take a stand for truth and honesty, we will be noticed. In so doing, we could lose jobs, lose promotions, or encounter conflict. The risk is worth it in order to protect our conscience and reputation. Surrender to Christ's lordship and trust Him to clarify your best plan of action.

LORD OF LIFE AND DEATH

AND HE HUMBLED YOU
AND LET YOU BE HUNGRY.
Deuteronomy 8:3

25
Hard Times:
Lordship When Life
Is on the Edge

The fairytale Christians. Everything seems to go right for them. They have exemplary children and nice homes. Status and postition come their way in both Christian and non-Christian circles. They look sharp and dress in style.

Then there are those whose every move ends in near calamity. Their finances are always low. They suffer health problems. They experience no job success. Their children rebel. Month after month their lives perch on the edge of crisis.

Why should life be so unfair and so unequal? Shouldn't God balance things out? Both of these types of Christians love and serve God. They both pray. Neither lives in rebellion or sin. Yet the circumstances of life are so different.

Perhaps I have described extremes. Certainly the wealthy,

talented, and successful Christians also bear great burdens and encounter sickness and failure. And if we look to the Third World, we see that the vast majority of Christians live with poverty, sickness, war, and injustice.

Hard times are part of the lot of every Christian. Some hide it well. Some possess the resources to seek help or cover the need. But at some point every Christian will find his or her life assaulted with trouble for which no apparent reason exists. It just comes—sickness, conflict, job struggles, suffering, the death of loved ones, and other traumas of life.

Why does God permit or even direct this? Deuteronomy 8:1-3 gives us a glimpse of God's purpose:

> All the commandments that I am commanding you today you shall be careful to do, that you may live and multiply, and go in and possess the land which the LORD swore to give to your forefathers. And you shall remember all the way which the LORD your God has led you in the wilderness these forty years, that He might humble you, testing you, to know what was in your heart, whether you would keep His commandments or not. And He humbled you and let you be hungry, and fed you with manna which you did not know, nor did your fathers know, that He might make you understand that man does not live by bread alone, but man lives by everything that proceeds out of the mouth of the LORD.

The children of Israel were poised to enter the Promised Land after forty years of wandering in the wilderness. The first generation that left Egypt had died because of their disobedience in refusing to enter the Promised Land the first time. Now the Israelites were to get a second chance. They were motivated to avoid their parents' disobedience. Moses explained God's purpose in all that happened so they would understand and not repeat their parents' errors. These simple principles apply today. They are frequently reiterated in the New Testament.

Remember God's leading. "Remember"—the key word of Deuteronomy. The Israelites were never to forget the lessons of Egypt and the wilderness. They were to regularly remember God's miraculous leading and provision. In the Old and New Testaments the accounts of Egypt and the wilderness wanderings are recalled again and again. Why? Because when things are going well, it is easy to say, "My power and the strength of my hand made me this wealth" (Deuteronomy 8:17).

The hymn words, "Count your blessings, name them one by one," represent significant theology. We must recount to ourselves and our children how God has led us and provided for us over the years. Remember!

That He might humble you. Pride is the overriding characteristic of the human race: pride of place, position, nation, and race; pride of person, family, accomplishments, and ideas. Humility is the archenemy and antithesis of pride. Pride exalts self; humility exalts God. Humility tops the list of God's character fruit for every Christian. Humility does not come naturally; it must be developed. The ultimate admission of humility is total dependence of God and total abandonment of reliance on self. The ultimate humbling to Israel was the absence of food for the multitudes of people wending their way through the wilderness, and then the strange appearance of manna six days a week. They were *forced* into dependence.

Hard times, when there is nowhere to turn but to God, humble us. In such times there is no provision but by His hand. We must swallow our pride and admit our need. Difficult circumstances both reveal and build character. Through them we experience humbling dependence in a new way. When this happens, we must never forget the lessons and the deep sense of helplessness of that time. God's plan for Israel's future was success and victory. But victory without humility is empty.

Testing to reveal obedience. Hard times are testing times. They test character, obedience, attitude, and spiritual depth. God tested Israel to see what was in their hearts and whether they would be obedient to His Word. Testing reveals the real person—not so much to God, for He knows us fully, but it reveals our hearts to ourselves and to others. The value of a believer's works are tested or revealed by fire (see 1 Corinthians 3:12-15). Peter also speaks of trials as a means of proving our faith as it is tested by fire (see 1 Peter 1:6-7). Testing is never pleasant, but it is necessary.

I often wonder how obedient I would be under real persecution. Would I still obey God while suffering the loss of freedom? I can only know that answer through testing. My engineering and space background has given me a great appreciation for testing before flying. Every part, every computer program, every design on a spacecraft must be tested at "worst-case" conditions to expose weaknesses and insure safety. The great Challenger disaster of 1986 shows the tragic results of ignoring proper testing procedures. Christians should relish testing so our weaknesses can be exposed and corrected. In Deuteronomy 8 the testing came from God to produce obedience. God also tests us—to produce obedience to His Word.

God allows hard times to drive us to Him and to His Word. God not only humbled Israel, but He let them be hungry. When they were hungry, He stepped in and miraculously fed them for forty years. All for a purpose—to deepen their understanding of true dependence on Him. He wanted them to know that their lives were not sustained by food alone.

When Jesus encountered the temptation in the wilderness He quoted Deuteronomy 8:3, "Man shall not live on bread alone, but on every word that proceeds out of the mouth of God" (Matthew 4:4). Every word. Not just a select few. The focus is on obedience to God's Word in the midst of trials.

We cannot be obedient to His Word if we do not know it. Believers who neglect the personal intake of Scripture have no true food in times of trouble. They flounder and shrivel spiritually, often in bitterness toward God. Hard times harden them, while obedient Christians are softened and deepened during difficulties.

Lest you despair because you have not previously been obedient, you still can turn to God and find refuge and rest. In trials He will sustain you and lead you to obedience.

We build our hope on the sure promises of God, which abound in Scripture. We cling to them, pray them back to God, and see God fulfill them. Yet many believers remain ignorant of those great promises and consequently lose their basis for hope. As we spend time with God in His Word, we need to search out and claim His promises for us. We can never be disappointed in God.

Will there be hard times? Most certainly. God will use hard times to draw us closer to Him, to make us dependent, to build our characters, and give us understanding. In the hard times let's experience the fullness of life under the lordship of Christ.

AND HIS DISCIPLES ASKED HIM, SAYING,
"RABBI, WHO SINNED, THIS MAN OR
HIS PARENTS, THAT HE SHOULD BE BORN BLIND?"
JESUS ANSWERED, "IT WAS NEITHER THAT THIS MAN
SINNED, NOR HIS PARENTS; BUT IT WAS IN ORDER
THAT THE WORKS OF GOD MIGHT BE DISPLAYED IN HIM."
John 9:2-3

26
Health:
The Reality of a Weak Vessel

As I write this, several of my friends are battling ill health. Bob Hopkins is suffering from cancer of the blood. His body's immune system is damaged, allowing other diseases to invade. Rod Sargent, Navigator vice president, continues his long battle with cancer. Joyce Bogue endures the pain of recovery from brain surgery. Another friend suffers as a diabetic. This list could be endless.

Young and old alike encounter the ravages of disease. They visit doctors, read health journals, experiment with natural cures, pray, ask for prayer—and experience the spectrum of results from death to cure. It almost seems random as to who rebounds to health. Where is God in all this? Does He not care? Can He not heal? *Will* He not heal?

Surely God is there, He does care, and He can heal. But His purpose for our lives goes far beyond health. He focuses on our character and our witness to the watching world. As with the blind man of John 9, God displays His work in us—but always with purpose.

Ill health tests our commitment to the lordship of Christ. Even when we have done all that we can to wisely guard our bodies, sickness or accidents will come—if not now, certainly in old age. How will we respond? In anger against God for not protecting us? In guilt, feeling that we are being punished? In despair or depression over our condition? As we wrestle with the problem, we will probably experience some of each emotion.

How *should* we respond to ill health?

First, remember that God created us for His glory and knows us from birth to eternity (see Psalms 139:13-16). God's perfect creation became marred by sin—and we reap the results in our bodies to this day. Certainly we are "fearfully and wonderfully made," but we are fragile. One doctor gave his advice on how to live a long life: "Eat healthy foods, get good exercise, and pick the right ancestors! And of the three, the latter is the most determinative." Our genetic inheritance influences our entire lives. Thus, we live in a certain state of inevitability. We can compensate for, but we cannot cancel, our history. Genetic history tells us something. Knowing it, we can take certain precautions in our lifestyle. For instance, a history of heart disease warns us to monitor and lower our cholesterol levels and watch our weight.

Another aspect of history affects our health. When we have abused our bodies with drugs, alcohol, overwork, or tension, we will pay the price. Some effects are permanent, particularly in the case of drugs.

Good health comes as a blessing from God. Therefore we should do all that we can to protect and preserve it. Our body is the temple of the Holy Spirit—a gift from God and a trust of stewardship. But to what extent should we focus on its care? What is prudent and what is presumptuous? Three needs of a healthy body cannot be ignored without consequence. We need *rest* to refresh and rebuild the body physically and emotionally. We need healthy *nutrition* to build and repair the body. We need moderate *exercise* to condition the body. Extremes in any of these areas leads to imbalance and a wrong focus.

Christians, like most Americans, rally around certain fads or extremes. Health foods and vitamin supplements can be an example of this. They certainly are not bad. We need to eat more wholesome food. A person will feel better and be more productive with a balanced diet. But we should try to avoid an excessive focus on diet and nutritional aids or pushing them on others.

Exercise requires similar balance. In excess it actually destroys the body. The lack of it can kill us and rob us of endurance. For some, exercise becomes compulsive. I must guard against that myself. I am a handball fanatic, and I make time for it no matter how busy my schedule is. I need to be careful to keep that interest in balance.

Both diet and exercise need surrendering to the lordship of Christ. What is our motive in trying to improve either one? To be healthy or to be beautiful? For many women the drive to stay beautiful or thin springs from a gratification of ego. Ego also drives men to stay fit and trim. Wrong motives constantly plague us. On the other hand, being overweight and out of shape is not a good testimony either.

The Apostle Paul spoke of the right motive: "I buffet my body and make it my slave" (1 Corinthians 9:27). We need discipline. Discipline of the body and discipline of the mind and spirit are closely related. The focus must center on the proper purpose—to glorify God, not to please our own egos. We surrender our egos completely to Jesus Christ's lordship.

We exercise discipline under His lordship.

Having done the best we can in discipline and care of the body, we can allow God to bring whatever disease He wishes into our lives. For even with the best of care illness will come.

How does sacrifice relate to preserving our health? In the nineteenth century missionaries packed their goods in caskets, knowing they were likely to die early of disease. The greatest missionary thrust in history during the nineteenth and twentieth centuries was fueled by men and women who willingly sacrificed their health. Surely such a spirit of sacrifice should characterize every believer.

Is some sacrifice foolishness rather than faith? Robert Murray MiCheyne said as he lay dying at a young age, "God gave me a message to bring and a horse to ride. Alas! I have killed the horse and cannot bring the message." In spite of his fervent spirit, he wore out. Many people have abused their bodies in good causes and paid the penalty in poor health. This is unwise. We must discern the balance between sacrifice and selfishness.

But how do we exercise faith? In 2 Corinthians 12:15, Paul asserted, "I will most gladly spend and be expended for your souls." Should we not be willing to take some risks and move beyond self-protection? As I write this, I am about to leave on a trip to a part of the world where disease and poor sanitation are quite common. I have taken the proper medical precautions. I will exercise care in eating and drinking to the extent that I do not offend the people I am visiting. The rest is in God's hands. I have become ill while traveling before and likely will again. Logic says that I would be more healthy staying home. But would I, if my health is truly in God's hands?

Someone wisely observed, "Most of the work in the world is done by people who are sick, tired, and overworked." Don't be easy on yourself, but do discipline yourself. Then willingly step out in faith.

One final word on a real health wrecker—stress. No matter how carefully you eat and exercise, unless you learn to moderate the levels of stress in your life, you will still open yourself to much illness and a shortened life. Dr. Archibald Hart states:

Recent research suggests that one way excessive stress causes illness is by destroying the body's immunological defense mechanisms. In other words, too much stress saps the body's ability to fight off disease, so that viruses and bacteria thrive. It doesn't do it immediately, nor totally. The process takes place slowly, eventually robbing us of just enough "fighting power" to place us at jeopardy for illness. There is even some suspicion that stress may cause some forms of cancer to grow more rapidly because the body's ability to fight off the growth of cancerous cells is destroyed or diminished.[1]

Stress results from our responses to many of life's circumstances—good and bad. Christ's lordship must also reign over these circumstances and our response to them.

We each will face ill health. Our attitude to this illness measures the depth of our surrender to Christ's lordship. For several years my wife battled high blood pressure. She jogged, kept her weight low, carefully guarded her diet and salt intake—and yet her blood pressure kept climbing. She prayed about her stress responses. Both of us joked, with some seriousness, that living with me would give anyone high blood pressure! Even the medication lost its effectiveness, and her heart started showing the effects. We were concerned—even frightened. One of the men in our couples' Bible study, Dr. John Ball, took on her case and discovered a rare type of tumor on her adrenal gland. After thorough confirmation, the gland and tumor were surgically removed. Mary's blood pressure dropped to normal and has continued to be normal without medication.

We learned that even the best diet and exercise did not prevent the illness due to the tumor. Through this illness we learned dependence on God and a willingness to live with whatever He put into our lives. Almost daily we praise God for her healing, but we also know that God's plan could have been quite different for us.

God is sovereign over our bodies. We exercise prudence and balance, and God determines the results. I like the comment of one of our Navigator staff men in a war-torn country: "We have decided that it is not how long we live that counts, but what we live for."

May God make purposeful living the focus of all our health concerns. And when ill health prevails, let us continue to praise Him and gladly live under Christ's lordship.

NOTE:
1. Dr. Archibald D. Hart, *Adrenalin and Stress* (Waco: Word, 1986), page 23. I recommend this book for its excellent, practical help in facing stress.

I AM EIGHTY-FIVE YEARS OLD TODAY.
I AM STILL AS STRONG TODAY AS I WAS
THE DAY MOSES SENT ME; AS MY STRENGTH
WAS THEN, SO MY STRENGTH IS NOW,
FOR WAR AND FOR GOING OUT AND COMING IN.
NOW THEN, GIVE ME THIS HILL COUNTRY.
Joshua 14:10-12

27
Retirement:
The Caleb Factor

Forty years a slave in Egypt, one dangerous mission as a spy whose report was summarily rejected, forty years of wandering in a wilderness as all his generation died, five years of fierce fighting to capture a new land—that should be enough work to build in any man a desire for a quiet retirement. But not Caleb. He asked for more: "Give me this hill country" (Joshua 14:12).

We need more Calebs. Where are they in today's society? The mentality among Christians and nonChristians is to retire and go to Arizona or Florida, or to go fishing, or to do "what I want to do."

This is dangerous thinking that reveals a life focused on self and security. Just at the time when work no longer squeezes a person into limited options, the tendency arises to escape and avoid spiritual involvements.

The greatest untapped missionary and spiritual work force in the United States is the population of retired men and women. For the first time in this century, the number of people over 65 exceeds those in their teen years. We are seeing the "graying of America." Add to this the earlier retirement, greater mobility, and greater longevity, and we see the potential of a dynamic population of men and women seeking meaning in life and usefulness to society. What an opportunity for evangelism! What an opportunity for service!

Christians who retire from their secular professions can meet a vast spectrum of needs in the church, in missions, and in local parachurch organizations. Most of these groups suffer from lack of finances and personnel. At the same time there are incredible untapped skills in the over-55 retired Christian population—accountants, managers, carpenters, attorneys, secretaries, craftsmen, teachers, and others with special skills. Additionally, these people possess spiritual gifts used for years on a part-time basis, which can now be used full-time.

These are not new ideas. Many godly men and women have done this for years, but only in small numbers. When Lt. General William K. Harrison retired from the U.S. Army, his life purposes remained intact—reaching people for Christ and teaching the Scriptures. He only increased the proportion of his time doing it. In our church, Herb Stadler has served for over 15 years of his retirement in helping maintain our facilities. Bob Hage, former executive vice-president of McDonnell-Douglas Corporation, serves with The Navigators in a continuing outreach to businessmen. Hank and Eileen Dawson now continue full-time with their outreach to servicemen in Phoenix, Arizona. Many others have gone for short terms to the mission field to construct buildings, develop agricultural projects, lend business or maintenance expertise, teach or counsel, and serve where needed.

You may ask, "Where does the lordship of Christ fit into this discussion?" It is central to the issue. It may mean surrendering that urge to "go to Arizona." It may mean a move away from children and grandchildren. It may mean not pursuing that hobby or building that cabin on the lake. It may mean allowing new demands on one's life rather than pursuing leisure.

Perhaps for years you have heard the cry of many needs, but your availability was limited. Now you can respond. You are available. You can go. You can give of your time and life. But are you willing to forego the dream of a life of ease in retirement? That is a lordship decision.

The opportunities are obvious, yet few respond. Why do people not flock to such obvious opportunities? The reasons are basic to all life decisions that ought to come under the lordship of Christ, but do not.

The first reason is *spiritual immaturity*. People who have been believers for many years may not have focused on personal spiritual growth. It becomes virtually impossible to suddenly focus in later years. There is too much pride, ego, and history.

Often there is *no inner drive* to serve God. At many turning points of life people ignored the prompting of the Holy Spirit, and now they are insensitive and unresponsive.

These people fulfill this sad picture:

For though by this time you ought to be teachers, you have need again for someone to teach you the elementary principles of the oracles of God, and you have come to need milk and not solid food. (Hebrews 5:12)

Do not be deceived. The issue is the deep impact of the Word in your life as you wrestle with personal application and issues of lordship, having "senses trained to discern good and evil" (5:14).

The second reason is the *absence of a life focus* other than job and family. A concern for ministry does not develop just because time suddenly becomes available. The inertia and momentum of past life direction propels us in the same direction as we were going. Ideally, the concerns and burdens for service to God should simply expand to fill the increased time available in retirement years. Thus, preparation for retirement needs to be started years ahead. Prepare to give yourself full-time to God's purposes.

The third reason is *selfishness*. After years of working for retirement we can lust after ease and leisure, thinking we have earned it. It is proper that we slow down if our health requires it, but are ease and leisure really a worthy goal? Many who retire into a vacuum die within months or a few years. Life without focus and purpose is literally deadly. Step out of yourself. Give yourself to a worthy goal. Don't just spend the rest of your life—invest it!

The final reason is *fear:* fear of failure, fear of change, fear of the unknown, fear of not being able to learn new things, fear of leaving security. In facing fear Caleb can be our example. He refused to quit; he set new goals and he stepped out in faith. He had seen the tragic consequences of fear as he watched his friends die in the wilderness. He knew he could never retire and sit on the sidelines. So he set out on a new challenge at age 85.

At the same time as we move ahead in faith, we should be realistic. Even when spiritual immaturity, lack of life focus, selfishness, and fear are overcome, many other obstacles impede. Many churches and other organizations are not geared to find a place for retired men and women. If a place is found, it is most often in a serving, not a leading, capacity. One's pride and ego can easily cause problems as younger, less experienced people lead and direct. Often health problems can prevent a full investment of one's abilities. The trauma of change in later years can be overwhelming.

In spite of many potential obstacles, God can and will use you. But you must make the first move. Start making plans as you enter your early fifties. Prepare yourself. Seek out opportunities. Intensify your personal ministry. Don't allow your life to wind down like a mechanical toy.

A dear friend, J. Oswald Sanders, has been a great example to me. At 83 he still speaks over 300 times per year in his fourth career. He was an attorney, then headmaster of a school, then director of Overseas Missionary Fellowship, and now continues to serve in a teaching ministry. He continues to yield fruit in old age.

Let's keep going to the very end, as long as health and mental capacity continue. There is no rest and no end in the spiritual battle. Don't wait—start now.

THE RIGHTEOUS MAN WILL FLOURISH LIKE THE PALM TREE. . . .
THEY WILL STILL YIELD FRUIT IN OLD AGE;
THEY SHALL BE FULL OF SAP AND VERY GREEN.
Psalm 92:12,14

28
Old Age

"It's no fun to be old," my mother-in-law said to me shortly before her death. She and her husband had moved to Colorado Springs to be near us. She was afraid to drive in the busy city traffic. They had no peer relationships. Her husband's health was failing. No, it was not fun.

Now my father-in-law is in a nursing home. We watch as daily he becomes more frail. His once long stride is reduced to short shuffling steps. His mind becomes confused. He knows it, and it embarrasses him. He is lonely and bored. His life consists of three meals a day and long hours of sleep. He lives from visit to visit with his family. Time and events all melt into confusion. Yet daily he reads the Scriptures and praises God for the health he does have. His attitude is great, but his loneliness is desperate.

One day we will all face similar events in our own lives. Living under the lordship of Christ in youth and vitality is one thing. Living under His lordship in old age is quite another matter.

As young people, we may have felt discomfort around older people, especially those who had become physically or mentally infirm. Few adults, of any age, find it easy to spend much time in a nursing home. There you find people who cannot speak, walk, or even feed themselves. Many find themselves abandoned by family. It seems that they just sit there waiting to die. It's not a pretty picture. It shatters all dreams of retirement and leisure. Yet it is real—and one day we may be there.

How do we respond to the lordship of Christ then? How we respond then will depend largely on how we respond now in our care and concern for the elderly.

Our Western civilization is one of the few cultures in existence today where the elderly have become "excess baggage." Such a view accompanies the general decline and deterioration of the family and our value system. Divorce and abandonment on one end spawn abandonment on the other. Our mobile society and rapid urbanization undermine family unity. We cannot turn back the clock, nor can we change our society. What can we do?

First, we need to understand the biblical view of old age.

God values all of life. No one segment of life is of more importance in God's view. God says, "I have loved you with an everlasting love" (Jeremiah 31:3). There is no partiality with God. He loves all—old and young.

The Scriptures teach us to treat the elderly with respect, kindness, and love: "You shall rise up before the gray-headed, and honor the aged, and you shall revere your God" (Leviticus 19:32).

Jeremiah condemned Israel because "elders were not respected" (Lamentations 5:12). Younger men and women are to respect and honor elder men and women. The Scriptures not only teach respect for our parents and grandparents, but also special care for them. This is part of the commandment to "honor your father and mother." We must not abandon them in their old age. Our responsibility to elderly parents and relatives is a major lordship decision.

As my father-in-law has become more dependent and forgetful, my wife and I have both recognized that one day we will be in the same circumstance. Then we ask, "How would I want to be treated in this situation?" Our children will observe how we treat and speak of our parents, and in due time we will reap what we have sown.

Will the lordship of Christ govern our lives in old age? It depends much on what a person thinks now. The inner character of a person in the 40-65 age span will be the outer person in old age. What has been bottled up inside will spill over, and with the ailments of old age inhibitions crumble. Not all elderly people are sweet, nice, and pliable. What will we be like? We will be like the inner thoughts of our hearts today.

In his confrontation with Job, Elihu compared youth and the wisdom of elders. Though he was rash, there is truth to his words.

> I thought age should speak, and increased years should teach wisdom. But it is a spirit in man, and the breath of the Almighty gives them understanding. The abundant in years may not be wise, nor may elders understand justice. (Job 32:7-9)

Age does not necessarily bring wisdom. Godliness and gray hair are not synonymous. Even in old age we need to

grow in wisdom and godliness. It may be that the deepest
spiritual work in your life will take place then.

Suppose we are approaching or are already in old age.
What choices of lordship should we make?

We need to surrender and resurrender our lives to His
lordship especially as we consider His sovereignty in bringing
us to this point of our lives. Health may fail, but He is still
our Lord—and He values us regardless of our physical condition.
We are of as much value to God in old age as when we were
in the prime of life.

Next, praise God for all of life. The key word of Deuteronomy is "Remember." "And you shall remember all the way
which the Lord your God has led you in the wilderness these
forty years" (Deuteronomy 8:2). "He is your praise and He is
your God, who has done these great and awesome things for
you which your eyes have seen" (Deuteronomy 10:21).

Even when our lives consist of hard times, in retrospect we
see God's gracious leading and provision. We can praise Him.
Praise will lift our hearts above the frailty of the years. "I will
sing to the Lord, because He has dealt bountifully with me"
(Psalm 13:6). Even though we recall times of stress, we know
that "He has not dealt with us according to our sins, nor re-
warded us according to our iniquities" (Psalm 103:10).

In praise we honor Him. In praise we draw on His strength
and power. Praise Him also for today's health, regardless of
its state. He still reigns as Lord of the body. "For He Himself
knows our frame; He is mindful that we are but dust" (Psalm
103:14). Praise will lift our spirits, for we cannot praise and
complain at the same time.

Ask God for a sweet spirit and attitude. Only in that state
can we continue to share the love of Christ. "And even when
I am old and gray, O God, do not forsake me, until I declare
Thy strength to this generation, Thy power to all who are to
come" (Psalm 71:18). Guard yourself from a harsh, demanding

attitude. Only God can help in this task, for the body and mind weaken, and control becomes more difficult. But God is sufficient. We share in His promise to Israel, "Even to your old age, I shall be the same, and even to your graying years I shall bear you! I have done it, and I shall carry you; and I shall bear you, and I shall deliver you" (Isaiah 46:4).

I love the story of the 96-year-old man who was being admitted to a nursing home. A social worker was interviewing him and asked, "Did you have a happy childhood?"

He replied, with a twinkle in his eye, "So far, so good!" What a great attitude!

In old age let God show the depth of character built through the years. Listen to Paul's description:

> Older men are to be temperate, dignified, sensible, sound in faith, in love, in perseverance. Older women likewise are to be reverent in their behavior, not malicious gossips, nor enslaved to much wine, teaching what is good, that they may encourage the young women. (Titus 2:2-4)

To the very end, your life can wield a great influence and encourage others. Never stop expecting God to use you. You can still bear fruit in old age. That is God's promise. Claim it today.

O DEATH, WHERE IS YOUR VICTORY?
O DEATH, WHERE IS YOUR STING?
1 Corinthians 15:55

29
Death:
Ultimate Human Reality

Death brings us face to face with reality. In death we see our ultimate end.

Recently I visited my mother's grave with my father. A few yards away there stood a young couple in the their late 20s. The young man's shoulders were shaking as he sobbed by a gravesite. His wife patted his back and tried to comfort him. In those moments of time the reality of death penetrated his heart and emotions in a way no other event can.

The emptiness and sorrow makes us view life in a new way. For some, grief turns into bitterness and stoic hardness. In others, the death of a loved one opens their hearts to God as the only hope of life—a life after death. For many believers it forever alters their system of values.

I vividly recall my mother's last days. As I sat in that sterile hospital room and watched her slipping away, I came to a new lordship commitment. I realized that much of my value system, even as a committed believer, was patterned after the world. God impressed my heart and mind in those days in a way that I now find difficult to describe. Two major conclusions emerged in that time: the only lasting values were people and the Word of God. All that I do must focus on those eternal values.

Was there still sorrow? Yes. The night of her death I wept uncontrollably in my bed, much to my surprise and in contrast to the stoic objectivity I had demonstrated up to that point. Mother knew Christ and was with the Lord. Still there was sorrow in the midst of hope, but the sorrow was a cleansing sorrow.

The Bible views death for a believer not as a tragedy, but as a transition. Death releases the Christian from the bonds and infirmities of the body to enter into the indescribable reality of eternal life.

So do we look forward to death? I think not. No one longs for death, except those who are suicidal or who are suffering great pain. As Christians, we intellectually admit death's blessedness in God's perfect timing. But when we are in good health and life is going well, we do not relish it at all.

I have sometimes heard Christians speak of their desire to be in Heaven and with Christ. I felt guilty because I did not share this deep feeling. I was having too much fun in this life—not in the world's ways either. I really enjoy life. As a committed Christian, I have purpose and reason to live. Life is a great challenge. I think believers have more to live for than anyone else. I do not want to die. But I will. Perhaps even today.

So how shall we view death? When an elderly person dies, there is sorrow, yet resignation that the "time had come." But when a baby or a young person in the prime of life dies, the loss seems tragic. We may feel that the young person was taken before his time. We may even be angry at God. But in God's eyes, the death of a 15-year-old is no more tragic than the death of an 80-year-old. Both are in God's plan and God's timing. If they are believers, both experience the same joy and glory of eternal life.

I do not wish to sound harsh. If one of my children were to die suddenly, I would feel a sorrow and loss deeper than I felt at my mother's death. For I, too, intuitively view long life better than shortened life. This view is also found in Scripture. Many passages describe long life as a sign of God's blessing, for example: "Honor your father and mother (which is the first commandment with a promise), that it may be well with you, and that you may live long on the earth" (Ephesians 6:2-3). Long life is a reward of obedience. Long life is to be desired as a blessing of God—but only if one walks righteously.

> Whoever of you loves life and desires to see many good days, keep your tongue from evil and your lips from speaking lies. Turn from evil and do good; seek peace and pursue it. (Psalm 34:12-14, NIV)

To fully grasp the meaning and implications of death we must understand its origin. Physical death is a direct result of sin. "But from the tree of the knowledge of good and evil you shall not eat, for in the day that you eat from it you shall surely die" (Genesis 2:17). This was a direct command from God to Adam and Eve. Satan questioned God's honesty when he said to Eve, "You surely shall not die!" (Genesis 3:4). So our ancient parents disobeyed, bringing sin and physical death into the world, as well as spiritual death. God said, "By the sweat of your face you shall eat bread, till you return to the ground, because from it you were taken; for you are dust, and to dust you shall return" (Genesis 3:19).

So sin brought death, and death became the destiny of every human. Human beings labor, knowing death will come, and how one views death determines how one lives. A person who, knowing the inevitability of death, sees nothing beyond and lives a life of wantonness and self-pleasure is like the writer of Ecclesiastes, who morbidly reflects:

So no one has power over the day of his death. . . . There is something else meaningless that occurs on earth: righteous men who get what the wicked deserve, and wicked men who get what the righteous deserve. This too, I say, is meaningless. So I commend the enjoyment of life, because nothing is better for a man under the sun than to eat and drink and be glad. (Ecclesiastes 8:8,14-15, NIV)

Author William Saroyan, who once wrote that "the best part" of a man "stays forever," died in 1981 after a two-year bout with cancer. Only five days before he was hospitalized he telephone the Associated Press to report that cancer had spread to several of his vital organs. He then gave this final statement to be used after his death: "Everybody has got to die, but I have always believed an exception would be made in my case. Now what?"[1]

So now what? That question rests almost unknowingly on the lips of every living person—believer and unbeliever. But for the believer there is hope. There is life after death for the one who receives the salvation and forgiveness Christ offers.

The believer's hopes are expressed repeatedly throughout the Scriptures. Death is viewed by God with joy: "Precious in the sight of the LORD is the death of His godly ones" (Psalm 116:15). In God we have confidence in time of death: "Even though I walk through the valley of the shadow of death, I fear no evil; for Thou art with me; Thy rod and Thy staff, they comfort me" (Psalm 23:4). Paul speaks of his own struggle: "But I am hard-pressed from both directions, having the desire to depart and be with Christ, for that is very much better; yet to remain on in the flesh is more necessary for your sake" (Philippians 1:23-24).

The biblical view is that God will bless in life or death:

> For not one of us lives for himself, and not one dies
> for himself; for if we live, we live for the Lord, or if
> we die, we die for the Lord; therefore whether we live
> or die, we are the Lord's. (Romans 14:7-8)

Best of all, after death we shall be with the Lord: "He shall wipe away every tear from their eyes; and there shall no longer be any death; there shall no longer be any mourning, or crying, or pain" (Revelation 21:4).

Yet even with this incredible hope, we experience sorrow, especially at the death of one who is young. Yet God knows the future and what is best for us and for that young person. A beautiful example is seen in the family of King Jeroboam. He was a wicked king upon whom God brought judgment. God found good only in one of his family, his son Abijah. And God permitted Abijah to die! Consider God's reason. He said to Jeroboam's wife:

> When your feet enter the city the child will die. And all
> Israel shall mourn for him and bury him, for he alone of
> Jeroboam's family shall come to the grave, because in
> him something good was found toward the LORD God of
> Israel in the house of Jeroboam. (1 Kings 14:12-13)

All the rest of the family were to die ignominious, tragic deaths. God rescued Abijah by death. God knows what is best.

As we wrestle with the reality of death, we are led to

the lordship of Christ over our lives. Death is a constant reminder that life is limited, a trust from the living God. We are stewards of our days. God knows our ways and our needs. We give Him glad permission to take us in His time. Or, like many of our brothers and sisters in great persecution, we ask Him to take us to be with Him.

Death holds no fear for the believer, yet our human mind loves life and clings to it. Only under His lordship can we reconcile the desire to live with the blessing of death.

We know a judgment of our works awaits us. That too leads us to live under His lordship in this life. Then we can exclaim with Paul:

"O death, where is your victory? O death, where is your sting?" The sting of death is sin, and the power of sin is the law; but thanks be to God, who gives us the victory through our Lord Jesus Christ. (1 Corinthians 15:55-57)

These stanzas of Henry Ware stir us to see our Lord and death in a new light.

Lift your glad voices in triumph on high,
For Jesus hath risen, and man cannot die.
Vain were the terrors that gathered around Him,
And short the dominion of death and the grave;
He burst from the fetters of darkness that bound Him,
Resplendent in glory, to live and to save.
Loud was the chorus of angels on high—
"The Saviour hath risen, and man shall not die."

Glory to God, in full anthems of joy;
The being He gave us, death cannot destroy.
Sad were the life we must part with tomorrow,
If tears were our birthright, and death were our end;

But Jesus hath cheered the dark valley of sorrow,
    And bade us, immortal, to heaven ascend.
Lift, then, your voices in triumph on high,
For Jesus hath risen, and man shall not die.[2]

NOTES:
  1. William Saroyan in "Personal Glimpses," *Reader's Digest* (December 1981), page 136.
  2. Henry Ware, "Lift Your Glad Voices," *The Christian Book of Mystical Verse* (Harrisburg, PA: Christian Publications, Inc., 1963), page 119.

LORD
TO THE
WORLD

GO THEREFORE AND MAKE
DISCIPLES OF ALL THE NATIONS.
Matthew 28:19

30
The Consuming Vision

Some have vision; others just see. Some dream of distant lands; others know nothing of them. Some live beyond themselves; others live within themselves. Some see souls in need; others see only their own need. Some sacrifice to reach out; others never sacrifice. Some care; others ignore.

What makes the difference between these spiritual "haves" and "have-nots"? The key is inner yielding to the lordship of Christ—not so much in character and personal holiness, but in perceiving God's ultimate purpose.

We read of missionaries like Hudson Taylor and William Carey and categorize them as heroes. They were not. They, with countless others, were ordinary people with a vision for the world. They believed God intended that the gospel reach the entire world. So they went.

We may fear that kind of vision, thinking we would then inevitably have to go. All should be willing, but not all should go. Some go, some pray, some give—but all need the same depth of personal vision.

Recently I spent an evening with Dr. James Yost, an anthropologist who served with the Wycliffe Bible Translators and their Summer Institute of Linguistics. Jim and his wife, Kathy, had spent about ten years living among the Waorani people of Ecuador (the Auca Indians first reached by Jim and Elisabeth Elliot and four other missionaries; the five men were slain by the Aucas). We watched a BBC public television documentary on this tribe. Their language is unrelated to any other known language. Many of the Waorani have been transformed by Christ. As Jim and Kathy described living in that primitive society, another friend asked how they could ever tolerate such conditions. Jim and Kathy both affirmed they would do it again to be able to help people know Christ and improve their lives. The Great Commission guided their vision and gave them reason to leave the comforts of Western civilization.

We all live under obligation to fulfill Christ's Great Commission. That is the consuming vision of the New Testament. It must also be ours. Often it does not stir us to any action. What is the problem?

Either Christians do not know that the Great Commission exists and is central to the Christian life, or they may know it exists, but willfully ignore its command, perhaps because of sin or worldly concerns. Or they may not believe it applies to them.

The Great Commission is Jesus Christ's command to believers of all time. The gospel is to be preached to all the nations (Luke 24:47). And each believer is to be His witness (Acts 1:8). Then those who respond to the gospel are to become mature disciples of Jesus Christ (Matthew 28:18-20 and Colossians 1:28). We cannot ignore these commands. We are all required to obey our Lord.

If living under the lordship of Christ means anything at all, it certainly means obedience to His commands. Especially it means obedience to this, His supreme command after His resurrection and prior to His ascension.

In the book of Revelation Christ the Lamb is praised with these words, "Worthy art Thou to take the book, and to break its seals; for Thou wast slain, and didst purchase for God with Thy blood men from every tribe and tongue and people and nation" (Revelation 5:9). Every tribe, every tongue, every people, every nation—all are to be reached. The task never ends, because we each have our own generation to reach. The entire population of the earth changes about every 60 years. Thus the task always remains before us. The victories of previous generations cannot suffice for us. We cannot look back to the "age of missions" and rationalize away the urgency of the task today. The demands and needs of missions in the future will be greater than ever before, because of a burgeoning world population and the closing of many countries to traditional missionaries. The call for men and women with "secular" skills will increase drastically.

What can we do to develop this consuming vision for the lost and the world?

First, understand the great commission and its implications. Be convinced that it is for all believers today.

Second, go before the Lord in prayer. Ask Him what He wants you to do. Tell Him that you are totally available for any part in this great task. This does not mean that you must volunteer for overseas missions. Simply tell God you are available for wherever He leads. That could include overseas missions, but to think only in terms of foreign missions warps our understanding of *every* believer's involvement, because not all can or should go overseas. Right now, surrender your life to Jesus Christ for the fulfillment of the Great

Commission wherever He leads.

Third, begin to pray for the world, country by country. Pray for specific missionaries and their needs—in your home country and abroad. I suggest using a set of World Prayer Cards, published by Operation Mobilization, which give a brief description of each country of the world and some strategic prayer requests.[1]

Make prayer a family project, reading prayer letters and praying at family meals.

Fourth, give your finances to missions. Whether personally or through the church, make sure that a significant portion of your giving goes to home and foreign missions. Your heart will be where your money is.

Fifth, develop personal contact with missionaries. Write to them. Invite them into your home during their furloughs. Help them whenever possible.

My final suggestions to help develop a heart for the great commission strikes a more personal chord. We need to personally witness to the lost. Neighbors, coworkers, and relatives need to know the Lord Jesus Christ. We need not be gifted evangelists to witness of Christ's love. Nor should witnessing be a sudden, impulsive grabbing of another's collar, force-feeding a gospel presentation or tract. Instead, in the normal course of life, always be "ready to make a defense to everyone who asks you to give an account for the hope that is in you, yet with gentleness and reverence" (1 Peter 3:15).

We desperately need a consuming vision. Without it, the Christian life becomes stale and listless, lacking purpose and direction. In its absence, the church turns inward and forfeits its only place in society, yielding to a rattling of harmless swords against the social forces of evil. A Great Commission without a proper focus on the lost of the world is no commission at all—much less a great one.

This consuming vision must grasp every believer, not just

pastors and missionaries. Unless it infuses the ordinary lay-
person, we shall never see true revival and a powerful church.
Such vision controls every action and task from work in the
office or factory to holy times of prayer. Once such a vision
is experienced, nothing else will ever satisfy the heart.

The thoughts penned by Frank Houghton summarize the
thrust of our consuming vision.

> Facing a task unfinished,
>   That drives us to our knees,
> A need that, undiminished,
>   Rebukes our slothful ease,
> We, who rejoice to know Thee,
>   Renew before Thy throne
> The solemn pledge we owe Thee
>   To go and make Thee known.
>
> Where other lords beside Thee
>   Hold their unhindered sway,
> Where forces that defied Thee
>   Defy Thee still today,
> With none to heed their crying
>   For life, and love, and light,
> Unnumbered souls are dying,
>   And pass into the night.
>
> We bear the torch that flaming
>   Fell from the hands of those
> Who gave their lives proclaiming
>   That Jesus died and rose.
> Ours is the same commission,
>   The same glad message ours,
> Fired by the same ambition,
>   To Thee we yield our powers.

O Father Who sustained them,
　O Spirit Who inspired,
Saviour, Whose love constrained them
　To toil with zeal untired,
From cowardice defend us,
　From lethargy awake!
Forth on Thine errands send us
　To labour for Thy sake.

NOTE:
1. World Prayer Cards are available from STL Books, P.O. Box 28, Waynesboro, GA 30830, or from STL Books, P.O. Box 48, Bromley, Kent, England.

AND SEEING THE MULTITUDES,
HE FELT COMPASSION FOR THEM.
Matthew 9:36

31
The Lost:
Does Anyone Care?

I have been blessed with excellent eyesight most of my life.
But people who have defective vision tell me what it is like.
Nothing is clear or distinct. Fuzziness surrounds them. They
cannot read road signs. Depending on the type of problem,
some must read a book held a few inches from their noses.
They are like the blind man who told Jesus, "I see people;
they look like trees walking around" (Mark 8:24, NIV).

Then these people describe their feelings when they first
put on glasses. My wife, Mary, put on her first pair of glasses
on the second floor of an optical shop in a little Minnesota
town. "Mother, I can read that sign down there!" she exclaimed.
People with new glasses see leaves on trees distinctly. They
view their friends and loved ones with features they had never

seen before. It is a new world for them.

With good eyesight, I could sympathize, but not empathize—until recently. First road signs began to blur when I drove at night. Then the edges of everything I looked at became fuzzy. I am now struggling to get used to bifocals. It's great to see clearly. In a small way I can now identify with those who have poor vision.

But if only there were glasses to sharpen spiritual sight for Christians. Things which are so obvious to some are not seen by others. Some Christians travel and see the sights. Other Christians travel and see the people—as they are—lost and helpless without Christ. Jesus traveled, "and seeing the multitudes, He felt compassion for them, because they were distressed and downcast like sheep without a shepherd" (Matthew 9:35-36). Jesus saw their real need—and responded.

What do we see when we look at people? Clothes? Social status? Customers? Nice people? Or do we see people who are lost and who have a great need?

Why do we not see the spiritual reality of peoples' lives? Because when we see, we then bear responsibility to respond, to become involved. Some people believe that everyone is saved. Then they have no responsibility for sharing the gospel. Many of us may truly believe people are lost, but our actions are little different, because we do nothing. Someone wisely said, "He who can read, but does not, is no better off than one who cannot read." To see the need of a lost world and do nothing is of no greater value than one who cannot see.

I call it selfish blindness. Who cares as long as our souls—and those of our families—are safe? We have "seen the light" but feel no burden for those in spiritual darkness.

How can believers who have experienced the healing of spiritual blindness ignore the needs of the world? The answer is neither simple nor easily understood. Satan always pitches his battle to keep the believer from reaching out to the lost.

There can be no true spiritual growth or depth apart from a clear conviction that men and women are eternally lost apart from personal belief in Christ. This truth strikes at the very nature of the gospel and the meaning and necessity of Christ's death on the cross. To believe otherwise degrades the person of Christ. Daily devotional times, knowledge of Scripture, warm fellowship, and prayer will not bear spiritual fruit if we deny the fact that people will be lost for eternity without Christ.

As a remedy, consider these ideas:

1. If you sense a spiritual blindness in your life, openly confess it to God. Ask Him to open your eyes to the real needs of people around you.

2. Review Scriptures on the fate of people without Christ: "For the wages of sin is death" (Romans 6:23). "He who believes in [Christ] is not judged; he who does not believe has been judged already, because he has not believed in the name of the only begotten Son of God" (John 3:18). Does God really mean what He says?

3. Write down the names of ten people to whom you are close who are lost. Use the word "lost." It is easier to use the word "nonChristian," but "lost" conveys the stark reality of their condition.

4. Ask yourself if you really care whether they are ever saved? How much do you care?

5. Now ask God to burden your heart for those people as individuals.

You are probably waiting for me to "drop the other shoe" and urge you to share Christ with them. I'd like to. But that is not the issue here. That is often the barrier to believing that people are lost. For to admit it fully is to be obligated to confront them. That is a second step, one that the Holy Spirit will enable you to do in His time.

The book of Revelation describes the fate of those who do not accept Christ:

> And I saw a great white throne and Him who sat upon it. . . .
> And I saw the dead, the great and the small, standing
> before the throne, and books were opened; and another
> book was opened, which is the book of life; and the dead
> were judged from the things which were written in the
> books, according to their deeds. . . . And death and Hades
> were thrown into the lake of fire. This is the second
> death, the lake of fire. And if anyone's name was not found
> written in the book of life, he was thrown into the lake of
> fire. (Revelation 20:11-15)

A horrible picture, yet it is true. A second death awaits those who die without Christ. Can we look out on the multitudes and, like Christ, feel compassion for them? Do we see through the facade of respectability and goodness to the central issue of all human existence? As we submit to the lordship of Christ, we submit to what He said about man being eternally lost without Him. Lord, help us truly to see.

> Give me a sight, O Saviour,
>   Of Thy wondrous love to me,
> Of the love that brought Thee down to earth,
>   To die on Calvary.
>
> O make me understand it,
>   Help me to take it in,
> What it meant to Thee, the Holy One,
>   To bear away my sin.
>
> Then melt my heart, O Saviour,
>   Break me, yes, break me down,
> Until I own Thee Conqueror,
>   And Lord and Sovereign crown.
>   —Katherine Agnes May Kelly

32
Association with Sinners:
Where Is the Battlefield?

The Monday morning quarterbacks replay each critical decision of the weekend's football game. "He missed such an easy pass." "He should have run this way." "The coach ought to be fired for that call." "Can you believe the stupidity of that play?" On it goes. Fat, lazy bystanders second-guessing the bruised, tired players. It's a national pastime, encouraged because it brings paying customers back to the game.

But life is not a game. Hell is not just losing a match, nor is Heaven winning. People are dying without Christ, eternally lost. To reach them demands a presence with them—daily and regularly, where they work, live, and play. Even football games cannot be won in the locker room—only in the dust of the playing field. We would jeer at a team that decided that the

177

camaraderie in the locker room—reliving the victories of the past—was more important than meeting the opponents on the playing field.

Believers must be with the lost in order to reach them. But to be with them in any meaningful way often draws the criticisms of certain Christian watchers. Jesus knew the feeling all too well. In Mark 2, He reached out to Levi, the hated tax collector. He ate in Levi's house. The religious watchers of the day saw it and promptly accused Him of eating with tax-gatherers and sinners.

Jesus' reply forms the watchword of all serious witnessing believers, "It is not those who are well who need a physician, but those who are sick. I have not come to call righteous but sinners to repentance" (Luke 5:31-32). The pattern of Jesus' life was "to seek and to save that which was lost" (Luke 19:10). In so doing Jesus was soundly criticized.

We must associate with the lost, but when we do, we can expect criticism from some Christians on two counts.

For one, we will not have enough time to participate in some of the activities that are considered standard for a dedicated Christian. Choices must be made. A choice to be with unbelievers will draw comment and criticism.

The second criticism will arise when we associate with nonChristians on their turf. Occasionally this will put us in compromising situations that may be misunderstood by the Christian community. Social gatherings and some sports events are key places where nonChristians engage in interactions of significance to their thinking apart from their jobs. But our witness is not to Christians, but to the lost.

I recently went to a birthday party a friend gave for his wife. It was not a sedate cake-and-punch affair. There were dozens of people, most of whom I did not know—and mostly nonChristians. My friends are new believers who have a large network of relationships in the community. There was abundant food, as well as a German music group playing accordion, clarinet, and trumpet.

A Christian friend of ours was at the party, and he commented, "I just hope they don't lose their nonChristian friends." When people become Christians, too often they cut themselves off from their nonChristian friends. They still know them, but they no longer remain real friends. The bridges of real-life communication have been destroyed.

Christian leaders often fill new Christian's lives with meetings, Bible studies, obligations, responsibilities—and warnings to avoid worldliness and to abandon any questionable activities and practices. We build a wall around them and change them in ways that make them unattractive to their former friends. We imprison them in the Christian community.

Sometimes, of course, drastic measures are necessary. Yesterday I met a man who is an alcoholic and who wrecked his life with drugs. For a time he needs isolation and all the Christian support he can get. He is fighting for his physical and spiritual survival. Others certainly need significant changes in their lives. But our methods of producing these changes often are like amputating a leg to cure a cut on the knee. We cure the cut and cripple the person for life. We must learn how to help people grow and bloom where they are planted, rather than uproot them and create a fruitless transplant.

We should not only tolerate, but encourage, close associations with nonChristians. This does not violate the teaching of separation and holiness of life. The classic passage on separation in 2 Corinthians 6:14-18 refers primarily to joining in worship of idols and false gods. There is to be no joining of spirit and fellowship in worship.

In 1 Corinthians 5, Paul emphasizes his intent:

> I wrote you in my letter not to associate with immoral people; I did not at all mean with the immoral people

of this world, or with the covetous and swindlers, or
with idolators; for then you would have to go out of the
world. But actually, I wrote to you not to associate with
any so-called brother if he should be an immoral person,
or covetous, or an idolater, or a reviler, or a drunkard,
or a swindler. (1 Corinthians 5:9-11)

Note that our separation is to be from sinning Christians,
not the lost. Clearly, we are to associate with the lost, because
they are our mission field.

Last year we had our Sunday school class to our home for
a Christmas party. But I asked everyone not to come if they
had an opportunity to go to an office party or a gathering
of nonChristians. We need to be where they are. Often the
Christian is not even invited to social functions, because they
have refused so many invitations. Have you ever hosted a
social gathering for your office? Do it. Make it a sumptuous
spread of food. Go the extra mile. We have, and it works.
While teaching at the Air Force Academy, we would host a
pregame brunch during football season. Open your house.
Go to their homes.

Another means of contact is to be sensitive to needs—
deaths, births, marriages—and extend yourselves in those times.
Take meals. Babysit for friends in the office who need that
help. You will be surprised at how closed doors open.

There is one other problem. We are particularly aggres-
sive to get a new believer into a "proper" church situation.
Don't rush them. Get them into the Word. Often it will take
one or two years for a new believer to feel comfortable in
an evangelical church environment. And if they are already
in another church, they won't easily leave their roots. Their
fellowship and teaching needs can be met in many other ways.
God grant that our motive is not to build our church membership or "count the scalps"—or even to hint that true conver-

sion means they come to our church.

When you decide to associate with sinners, you will be criticized. Take the risk. Step out in faith, and help others do the same. The world will never be the same because of your decision. At least you will be in the game, not in the grandstands. There, in the midst of the lost, Christ's lordship becomes more real than ever before.

HOW IS IT THAT YOU, BEING A JEW,
ASK ME FOR A DRINK
SINCE I AM A SAMARITAN WOMAN?
John 4:9

33
Crossing Cultures:
The Poison of Prejudice

Prejudice, racism, bigotry, nationalism—these ugly words describe the way most of the world thinks. The world is not fair. It never has been.

Christians can be guilty of similar thinking. We succumb to cultural forms that imprison our minds and emotions. None of these—prejudice, racism, bigotry, nationalism—can exist apart from a root of hatred and a large dose of pride and ego. Even we who abhor these attitudes find it difficult to practice what we preach. The traditional attitudes of our families and nations invade our actions in subtle ways.

The Christian, living in submission to the lordship of Christ, must think and live above culture, above race, above nationality. The Bible and the gospel are cross-cultural, but we have so often exported the message in cultural covers that have shielded the truth. When we export our culture along with the gospel, the gospel becomes blurred, and "nominal" Christians result—people who practice the imported forms, but are not converted.

Jesus always crossed the barriers of His time—the Sabbath, dining with taxgatherers, touching lepers, and talking with a Samaritan woman (John 4:1-42). The Samaritans, hated by the Jews in a centuries old confict, were the whipping boys of the time. They were dirt under the feet of the Jews.

The disciples had gone to the town to buy food. Jesus, tired from the journey from Judea, sat down by Jacob's well. A woman of Samaria came to draw water. He asked her for a drink. Being quick and sharp tongued, she answered, "How is it that you, being a Jew, ask me for a drink since I am a Samaritan woman?"

Then follows a most amazing conversation. "If you knew the gift of God, and who it is who says to you, 'Give me a drink,' you would have asked Him, and He would have given you living water." Nothing like a riddle to get attention!

"Sir, You have nothing to draw with and the well is deep; where then do You get that living water?" the woman asked. She was intrigued—living water!

"Everyone who drinks of this water shall thirst again," Jesus said, "but whoever drinks of the water that I shall give him shall never thirst; but the water that I shall give him shall become in him a well of water springing up to eternal life."

"Sir, give me this water, so I will not be thirsty, nor come all the way here to draw," the woman replied.

"Go, call your husband and come here," said Jesus.

"I have no husband."

"You have well said, 'I have no husband'; for you have had five husbands, and the one whom you now have is not your husband," Jesus said. He could have added that she was at the well at midday because she was unwelcome at the town well during the morning and evening hours when the women traditionally drew water.

The woman replied, "Sir, I perceive that You are a prophet."

Then followed a discussion on the proper place to worship. Jesus concluded by saying, "An hour is coming, and now is, when the true worshipers shall worship the Father in spirit and truth; for such people the Father seeks to be His worshipers. God is spirit, and those who worship Him must worship in spirit and truth."

She then shared her heart. "I know that Messiah is coming (He who is called Christ); when that One comes, He will declare all things to us."

Then the great revelation: "I who speak to you am He."

When the disciples returned, aghast that Jesus was speaking with a Samaritan woman, they feared to say anything. Yet through this outcast woman many of the townspeople believed in Christ.

What if Jesus had caved in to the traditional attitudes about women, Samaritans, and immoral conduct? It is significant that Jesus made His first and most direct revelation of Himself in this cross-cultural context.

As believers, we face two problems in communicating the gospel across cultural lines. The first is the commitment to erase personal prejudice and racial and national thinking from our lives. Paul declared, "There is neither Jew nor Greek, there is neither slave nor free man, there is neither male nor female; for you are all one in Christ Jesus" (Galatians 3:28). We must be fully convinced that God is no respecter of persons; He "is not one to show partiality" (Acts 10:34).

The natural man inside us rebels at such an idea. All history shows that people are not equal and that one always rules over another. Family backgrounds and geographical-cultural heritage teach us to hate—or at least dislike—those who are not like us. When we become Christians, we submit to Christ's lordship over prejudice, race, bigotry, and nation. Christ broke the barriers. So must we. We accept others unconditionally, but we cannot demand that we be accepted in return. No one can make this change in the flesh, only in the heart, because prejudice is a fierce enemy.

We cross the culture barrier to our neighbors, employees, townspeople, the poor in our cities, and the ethnic minorities in our midst.

The second problem is the cultural baggage we place on the gospel—both from the culture of our society and from the peculiar Christian culture built up over the years. Both cultures, secular and sacred, must be stripped to expose the truth of salvation.

In the Western world Christianity has become associated with forms and practices that help us worship, but which bear no mandatory mark of Scriptural authority. They are not wrong; they simply are one expression of our faith. The order of worship, the frequency of meetings, our music and style of preaching are all forms that must be rethought in light of Scripture, the clear communication of the gospel, and the new culture. History shows that Christians have often confused forms, legalism, and the gospel. We feel comfortable when things look "as they ought," while new converts puzzle over them and may easily miss the essence of the gospel, if not reject it outright.

We can confuse new believers—and worse, nonbelievers—about the true meaning of the gospel message. They see outward forms that, in an increasingly secularized society, are unfamiliar and meaningless. Just the plethora of denominations would confuse any thinking nonChristian.

We should be ready to abandon our Christian forms, if they are a barrier to the gospel. We should ask whether they are really needed or simply traditions. We need to do more than tolerate or accept others. We must cross the line into their frame of reference. Reaching out to Samaritans is risky because they live next door. Other Christians will see you with them and misunderstand your involvement with them. Paul understood this principle.

> And to the Jews I became as a Jew, that I might win Jews; to those who are under the Law, as under the Law, though not being myself under the Law, that I might win those who are under the Law; to those who are without law, as without law, though not being without the law of God but under the law of Christ, that I might win those who are without law. To the weak I became weak, that I might win the weak; I have become all things to all men that I may by all means save some. (1 Corinthians 9:20-22)

Paul was not a wishy-washy person. He was tough as nails, but on the right issues.

Who are the Samaritans in your life? When did you last ask them for a drink of water? or go to their house? or listen to them? or understand their feelings?

Do you remember that other Samaritan? The good Samaritan of Luke 10? Even Samaritans do commendable things. Christ commended them. Shouldn't we?

Prejudice is one of the greatest barriers to the gospel. Whether across nations or across backyard fences, it paralyzes effective evangelism. Before we condemn racial and social injustice, we should first examine our own lives and tear down the walls we have built. Then we will be able to share the true gospel with our neighbors and friends—and people in distant lands.

WERE NOT OUR HEARTS BURNING
WITHIN US WHILE HE WAS
SPEAKING TO US ON THE ROAD?
Luke 24:32

34
The Fellowship of
the Burning Heart

Have you ever read the Bible and felt like you were chewing
on leather—lots of chewing but no nourishment? I have, and I
didn't like it.

Then there are those special times when truth leaps out
of the Scripture and grips my heart. The reality of the person of Christ overcomes me and encourages me.

What makes the difference? I wish I could open my Bible,
feed a program into some heavenly computer, and get that
great experience every time. But life with our Lord is not
like that. We are not robots, and God is not seated at a computer terminal. He brings understanding in unusual ways.

He brought understanding on the road to Emmaus. The
disciples were in a state of shock. Jesus was dead. The rumors

of His resurrection seemed like nonsense. Despair and fear gripped them daily. On the seven-mile walk from Jerusalem to Emmaus, two depressed disciples relived the events of the past days. A man approached them and began to walk along with them. It was Jesus, but the disciples did not recognize Him.

Jesus asked, "What are these words that you are exchanging with one another as you are walking?" (Luke 24:17). They stopped and looked at Him.

Their eyes were reddened from tears, and sorrow etched their faces. They were amazed that this person was unaware of the events of the weekend. Jesus asked them to explain—which they did, expressing their disappointment in Jesus: "But we were hoping that it was He who was going to redeem Israel." They recounted the discovery of the empty tomb and the conversation of the angels with the women.

Then Jesus spoke quietly, but with gentle power.

"O foolish men and slow of heart to believe in all that
the prophets have spoken! Was it not necessary for the
Christ to suffer these things and to enter into His glory?"
And beginning with Moses and with all the prophets,
He explained to them the things concerning Himself in
all the Scriptures. (Luke 24:25-27)

The disciples still did not know it was Jesus. They invited Him to eat with them. At the table Jesus took the bread and blessed it. As He broke the bread and gave it to them, suddenly their eyes were opened, and they saw that it was Jesus.

Then He vanished from their sight!

After some shocked confusion, they said, "Were not our hearts burning within us while He was speaking to us on the road, while He was explaining the Scriptures to us?" A burning heart. A heart set on fire by the Lord Himself as He breaks the Word to us. That is what we all want. We want Jesus to come alongside as we walk and open our hearts and minds.

As we reflect on this account, a host of questions come to mind. Why didn't they recognize Jesus? The Scripture says their eyes were prevented from recognizing Him. Before we doubt this, recall how many times we failed to sense God's presence, and yet in retrospect we realize that He was present and in control.

What opened their eyes? Perhaps it was the similarity of the last meal with Christ in the upper room where He broke the bread and said, "This is My body, which is given for you" (Luke 22:19).

What opens our eyes? A memory of a particular time with the Lord? A painful circumstance? A sense of helplessness? God can use each of these as He wishes. Whatever the circumstances of the moment, eventually God through the pressure of His Word and His Spirit opens our eyes. That understanding brings a burning heart, the sure knowledge that God is speaking. It is not just an emotion, but a sense of the Scriptures coming alive in one's heart and mind.

God obviously wants us to consistently exercise this union of understanding and heart in His Word. How does it happen and what prevents it? Christ's lordship over His Word is expressed in two ways—His insistence upon obedience as evidence of humility, and secondly, through the Holy Spirit as the One who reveals the Scriptures to the believer.

Twice in Luke 24, Jesus "opened their eyes to understand the Scriptures." After Pentecost, that task belongs to the Holy Spirit. The Spirit continuously exercises that charge.

But the Helper, the Holy Spirit, whom the Father will send in My name, He will teach you all things, and bring to your remembrance all that I said to you. (John 14:26)
But when He, the Spirit of truth comes, He will guide you into all the truth; for He will not speak on His own

initiative, but whatever He hears, He will speak; and He will disclose to you what is to come. (John 16:13)

The Spirit reveals the Scriptures to us, not just in knowledge, but in understanding.

The Spirit, who indwells every believer, always stands ready to reveal the Word to us. We frequently lack His touch as we delve into Scripture. We must constantly make way for the Spirit to work.

The Spirit reveals the Word to a *cleansed* believer. Is there unconfessed sin which prevents the vessel of your life from being holy?

The Spirit reveals the Word to the *obedient* believer. Why should God bother to reveal further truth to those who spurn the truth they already have? Obey what you know.

The Spirit reveals the Word to the *prepared* believer, the one who is prepared and willing to obey any new revelation from the Scriptures.

The Spirit reveals the Word to the *hungry* believer—not the one who simply hungers for more knowledge, but the one who hungers for righteousness, whose heart longs for the intimacy with God that He promises.

Something may still be lacking. There can be no disclosure without the investment of time in the Scriptures. A brief devotional glance to salve the conscience will not do. Depth comes from digging in His Word—a metaphor that suggests both time and effort. No one will experience the fellowship of the burning heart without hours spent walking with Christ in His Word. There is no substitute or shortcut.

Those who are committed to a disciplined study of God's Word will be able to say with Paul,

Now we have received, not the spirit of the world, but the Spirit who is from God, that we might know the things freely given to us by God. . . . For who has known the mind of the Lord, that he should instruct Him? But we have the mind of Christ. (1 Corinthians 2:12,16)

Join the fellowship of the burning heart.

IS IT NOT TO SHARE YOUR FOOD WITH THE HUNGRY
AND TO PROVIDE THE POOR WANDERER WITH SHELTER—
WHEN YOU SEE THE NAKED, TO CLOTHE HIM,
AND NOT TO TURN AWAY FROM YOUR OWN FLESH AND BLOOD?
Isaiah 58:7 (NIV)

35
The Poor:
Whose Responsibility?

I walked through a hotel in Maui, Hawaii. Everywhere I turned there was the scent of wealth. Terraces, brilliant tropical birds, and ornately designed pools of water abounded. The hotel shops glittered with expensive goods. As I walked I began to feel more and more uncomfortable. I was not staying there, but it was more than a feeling of being an outsider. It was a sense that I did not belong there. It was too much, too rich. As I left, I almost felt ill. The contrast with this wealth and what I know of most of the world (even in the United States) was getting to me.

Then it occurred to me. The hotel was far beyond my lifestyle. But my personal lifestyle and standard of living would seem just as awesome to most of the world's population. It's simply a matter of degree. Most of the people in the world are poor as well as oppressed.

Where does the lordship of Christ lead the believer in regard to the poor of this world?

The Scriptures say much about the poor and God's concern for them. In the Old Testament God commanded protection and special care for the poor. Through Isaiah God said:

> Is it a fast like this which I choose, a day for a man to humble himself? Is it for bowing one's head like a reed and for spreading out sackcloth and ashes as a bed? Will you call this a fast, even an acceptable day to the Lord? Is this not the fast which I chose, to loosen the bonds of wickedness, to undo the bands of the yoke, and to let the oppressed go free and break every yoke? Is it not to divide your bread with the hungry, and bring the homeless poor into the house; when you see the naked, to cover him; and not to hide yourself from your own flesh? (Isaiah 58:5-7)

God ties a promise to our concern for the poor.

> And if you give yourself to the hungry, and satisfy the desire of the afflicted, then your light will rise in darkness, and your gloom will become like midday. And the Lord will continually guide you, and satisfy your desire in scorched places, and give strength to your bones; and you will be like a watered garden, and like a spring of water whose waters do not fail. (Isaiah 58:10-11)

God is deeply concerned. We are also to be concerned for the poor and helpless. When Jesus Christ began His ministry, one of the first passages He read about Himself was from Isaiah 61:1.

The Spirit of the Lord is upon Me, because He anointed
Me to preach the gospel to the poor. He has sent Me to
proclaim release to the captives, and recovery of sight
to the blind, to set free those who are downtrodden,
to proclaim the favorable year of the Lord. (Luke 4:18-19)

Jesus loved and ministered to the poor. He never turned
them away.

At this point the discussion could turn to a plan for the
church or a community to rescue the poor and erase poverty.
Jesus did not take this approach. He did not condemn the
system of government that spawned poverty or oppressed the
poor. Injustice ought to be attacked wherever it is found,
but Jesus' concern was ultimately for their salvation and immediately for the individual in need. His lordship in our
lives demands a response to the poor. But what response? We
seem so helpless in a world of oppression where the poor
become poorer.

We first need to develop a heart of *compassion,* "And
so, as those who have been chosen of God, holy and beloved,
put on a heart of compassion" (Colossians 3:12). Through the
psalmist God describes the righteous king: "He will have
compassion on the poor and needy, and the lives of the needy
he will save" (Psalm 72:13). Jesus looked at the multitudes
of people and "felt compassion" (Matthew 9:36).

Compassion is more than knowledge or information. It is
feeling with the poor as though we were there. It is sensing a
deep personal concern for their plight. The word means "with
feeling." Here emotion is an asset. But we become so hardened
to the poor in our midst—tending to blame their poverty on
laziness or lack of education. We soon become oblivious to
the poor, locking ourselves in our own comfortable world.

One of the means God used to open my eyes to poverty
was traveling in Asia. Something happened inside me when

I saw the poor of Calcutta—the destitute sleeping in the streets, the cardboard shacks, and the daily "dead wagon" to cart off those who died. In Sri Lanka I stayed in a poor home where a friend and I were fed separately from the family, who ate what we left. That left its mark. The masses of China, Indonesia, and the Philippines are poor in every sense of the word. Famine in Africa seems nearly unsolvable—an ongoing tragedy. We must allow our hearts to be touched with compassion.

Our next response is to *give.* I believe each of us should be giving some portion of our regular offering to meet the direct needs of the poor. We can do this through reputable organizations that work to relieve poverty. We also need to communicate the needs of the poor to our children. You may want to skip a meal a week and give what you would have spent. Or simply fix a simple meal of rice and vegetables, giving what you saved.

Then we come to the obvious: meet the needs of the poor where you live. They are there. Provide food and clothing. Stimulate your church to reach out. Support mission churches in poverty areas. Most ministries to ethnic minorities in the United States (especially black and Hispanic) find it almost impossile to survive on internal funding; the money simply is not there. We need to develop a burden for them and give generously.

My final suggestion relates to meeting the spiritual, as well as the physical, needs of the poor. Foreign missions sponsored by believers will seek to communicate the gospel as well as to meet physical needs. When people are converted, many are freed from superstition and bondage which locked them into poverty. One friend of ours in an African country taught people how to plant and harvest crops while he shared the gospel. Individually, he has done more to fight famine in the long-term than many large agencies.

But missions are expensive. In the last two decades the

cost of missions has escalated, particularly as more missions have had to focus on an increasingly unevangelized world in large cities. I can see no end in sight to that escalation. I would like to see every church direct fifty percent of its budget toward home and foreign missions. It may delay buildings and internally funded programs. It may trim church staffs. But the investment would give a new level of spiritual vitality to the church, a new vision for the world. Consider sending lay people in their professions to countries closed to missionaries. Such jobs often do not pay enough to support these persons, so churches will need to supplement their income.

God protect us from the complacency of our abundance while a world passes in poverty. We can't do everything, but we can do something. The believer truly under the lordship of Christ will not stand idly by. There is too much to do.

DECIDING
FOR
LORDSHIP

36
Putting Lordship
into Practice

Now what? Your mind and heart have been stimulated and convicted. You know the issues. Now comes the hard part—applying them to your life. Without application, this whole effort is little more than an academic exercise. Here are some specific ways to put lordship decisions into practice.

1. Don't try to change several areas at once. Deal with issues one at a time. Make a list of the areas about which God convicts you as you read His Word.

2. Deal first with clear issues of sin. Confess them and make a lordship commitment regarding them.

3. When you make a decision, write it down and attach a Bible verse to it. Memorize that verse and make a note, including the date, in the margin of your Bible.

4. Share your decision with someone else for accountability. Be specific on the decision, and specific on the accountability you want from them.

Lordship decisions are a constant process of living the Christian life. However, many people experience one or two very major lordship decisions in life and several smaller ones. The major lordship decisions are made very deliberately, often out of a crisis or a major life need. The smaller lordship decisions usually deal with specific issues.

Deuteronomy 8:2 instructs, "remember all the way which the Lord your God has led you." I suggest that you use the form at the end of this chapter to record the lordship decisions you have made. Add to it as you grow. Make a copy of the page and keep it in your Bible as a reminder.

May God richly encourage you and deepen your life as you grow in the lordship of Christ.

HISTORY OF LORDSHIP DECISIONS

	Date	Decisions, Circumstance, and Result	Key Verse
1.	_____	_____	_____
		_____	
		_____	
2.	_____	_____	_____
		_____	
		_____	
3.	_____	_____	_____
		_____	
		_____	
4.	_____	_____	_____
		_____	
		_____	
5.	_____	_____	_____
		_____	
		_____	

Examples:

1. September I realized that I had never turned my life   Luke
   10, 1984   fully over to Christ's lordship. I got on my   14:25-33
              knees and yielded myself to Christ's lord-
              ship. This caused a major change in my life.
              My entire Christian life began to take on
              new meaning. I shared this with my wife.

2. August 21, I have really struggled with greed. In study   Luke
   1985   I realized Christ was not Lord in this area.   12:15
              I made a lordship decision to surrender
              my possessions and money to Him. I in-
              creased my giving and sold three items that
              I had because of my greed. Asked Sam to
              ask me weekly how I am doing.

For Further Reading

Chapter 10

Petersen, J. Allan, *The Myth of the Greener Grass,*
Tyndale House Publishers, 1983.

White, Jerry, *Honesty, Morality, and Conscience,*
NavPress, 1978.

White, John, *Eros Defiled: The Christian and Sexual Sin,*
InterVarsity Press, 1979.

Chapter 12

Crabb, Lawrence J., Jr., *Effective Biblical Counseling,*
Zondervan Publishing House, 1979.

Crabb, *The Marriage Builder,* Zondervan Publishing
House, 1982.

Chapter 19
   Mayhall, Carole, *Words That Hurt, Words That Heal,*
   NavPress, 1986.

Chapter 24
   Mattson, Ralph, and Miller, Arthur, *Finding a Job You
   Can Love,* Thomas Nelson Publishers, 1982.
   White, *Honesty, Morality, and Conscience.*
   White, Jerry and Mary, *Your Job: Survival or Satisfaction,*
   Zondervan Publishing House, 1977.

Chapter 25
   Schaeffer, Edith, *Affliction,* Fleming H. Revell, 1979.

Chapter 26
   Hart, Archibald D., *Adrenalin and Stress,* Word, Inc., 1986.
   Schaeffer, *Affliction.*

Chapter 27
   Sanders, J. Oswald, *Your Best Years,* Moody Press, 1982.

Chapters 31 and 33
   Aldrich, Joseph, *Lifestyle Evangelism,* Multnomah
   Press, 1981.
   Mainhood, Beth, *Reaching Your World: Disciplemaking
   for Women,* NavPress, 1986.
   Petersen, Jim, *Evangelism as a Lifestyle,* NavPress, 1980.
   Petersen, *Evangelism for Our Generation,* NavPress, 1985.